Wh ... bi Yonassan
Ge

"... he [Gershom] is certainly a dynamic force to be reckoned with, bringing, as he does, many new ideas and concepts to the subject of reincarnation."

Roy Stemman, editor, *Reincarnation International,* London, Issue No. 4, November 1994.

"*Beyond the Ashes*... builds bridges among secular, political, and metaphysical realms. The seemingly effortless way in which Rabbi Gershom accomplishes so monumental a task pays tribute to his depth of knowledge and of a wisdom that was born of having transcended the very ashes of which he writes."

Amy Shapiro, book review, *Journal of Regression Therapy,* 1994, pp. 103-104.

"Rabbi Gershom addresses the Jewish traditional beliefs about the afterlife, all of which are important perspectives to be aware of for those willing to explore metaphysical issues... His presentation is compelling."

Carole Clark, book review, *The Association for Past-Life Research and Therapies, Inc., Newsletter,* Spring 1966, vol. 16, number 2.

"In this wonderful book, Rabbi Gershom and his fourteen fellow storytellers express the kind of unconditional love that can heal the painful soul memories of past lives, the anguish of those who continue to suffer in their present life experiences... I wholeheartedly recommend this book."

Brad Steiger, author of *Returning from the Light,* from his preface to *From Ashes to Healing.*

From Ashes to Healing

From Ashes to Healing

Mystical Encounters with the Holocaust

Fifteen true stories
collected and annotated by

Rabbi Yonassan Gershom

A·R·E PRESS
ASSOCIATION FOR RESEARCH AND ENLIGHTENMENT

A.R.E. Press • Virginia Beach • Virginia

2nd Printing, August 1997

Printed in the U.S.A.

A.R.E. Press
Sixty-Eighth & Atlantic Avenue
P.O. Box 656
Virginia Beach, VA 23451-0656

Library of Congress Cataloging-in-Publication Data
Gershom, Yonassan, 1947-
From ashes to healing : mystical encounters with the Holocaust : fifteen true stories collected and annotated / by Yonassan Gershom.
p. cm.
Includes bibliographical references.
ISBN 0-87604-340-6
1. Reincarnation—Biography. 2. Reincarnation therapy—United States. 3. Transmigration—Judaism. 4. Mysticism—Judaism. 5. Holocaust, Jewish (1939-1945). 6. Cabala. 7. Gershom, Yonassan, 1947- . I. Gershom, Yonassan, 1947- .
BL519.F76 1996
296.3'3-dc20 96-17356

Dedicated to the memory of
Rabbi Shlomo Carlebach,
whose music helped renew
the joys of Jewishness

Contents

Preface

I very much admired Rabbi Yonassan Gershom's earlier work, *Beyond the Ashes: Cases of Reincarnation from the Holocaust* (A.R.E. Press, 1992). The remarkable phenomenon of so many men and women experiencing a karmic link with the Holocaust—and so many of them non-Jewish folk from America's heartland—made for fascinating reading while establishing a solid case for reincarnation. I was most impressed with the documentation of the case studies in the book, and I was in awe of Rabbi Gershom's formidable scholarship.

During a telephone conversation soon after I had read *Beyond the Ashes,* Rabbi Gershom told me that his next book would deal more extensively with the healing of body, mind, and spirit, which very often occurs after the recall of a past-life experience as a Holocaust victim.

When I received the manuscript of *From Ashes to Healing: Mystical Encounters with the Holocaust,* I was honored by the accompanying letter that informed me that I was to be the first—outside of the able editor Jon Robertson—to read the work.

I sat down to glance through the manuscript about 2:30 A.M., just to get a preliminary feel for the book. When next I glanced at my wristwatch, it was nearly 5:30!

So firmly had the various accounts gripped me that I had been unable to put the book down until I finished it. The stories in this book are absolutely compelling and totally absorbing.

Indeed, Rabbi Gershom's meticulous scholarship is still very much in evidence, but he ably proves his contention that he is first and foremost a Hasidic storyteller. The case histories in *From Ashes to Healing* are presented in a manner that could hardly be surpassed for sheer drama and the evocation of emotional response in the reader. Throughout the text, Rabbi Gershom reveals himself as an individual of loving intent and unfailing good will.

From Ashes to Healing should, in my view, be as valuable as a teaching instrument, as it will undoubtedly be one of healing. As was the case with *Beyond the Ashes*, this book will build a solid bridge among people of widely diverse backgrounds.

Although I pride myself on my knowledge of world religions and metaphysics, I will freely admit that in Rabbi Gershom's two fine books I learned enormous amounts of information about Jewish traditions and Jewish theology of which I was previously unaware. And I will contend with little fear of contradiction that a good many of my Jewish friends would be as enlightened as I about certain aspects of Jewish belief structures. It would, in fact, come as a great shock to most of them to find out that Judaism has many teachings about the subject of reincarnation.

An aspect of the book which greatly intrigued me has to do with the presentation of the "ethnic soul," the concept that many soul entities may incarnate exclusively—or nearly so—in one tribal, religious, spiritual, or cultural tradition. Central to the understanding of a number of the accounts in this book is the idea of *yiddishe neshamah*, the "Jewish soul."

"Briefly stated," Rabbi Gershom explains, "Jewish mysticism teaches that the souls of the Jews who were present at Mt. Sinai (when the Torah was revealed) will continue to be Jewish for all incarnations, even if they are born into non-Jewish bodies."

Examples are given of certain individuals who, at first very confused by their ostensible memories of being Jewish and having been murdered in the Holocaust, later discover that they had Jewish ancestors, long forgotten in the amalgamation process of America's melting pot society.

If I have learned anything in my forty years as an author of over one hundred books on the paranormal and metaphysics, it is to maintain an open mind. While some souls may achieve their spiritual evolution by participating in numerous cultural expressions, others may evolve as steadily—or even more directly—by repeated incarnations in the same ethnic group.

Interestingly, I have heard a number of Native American shamans express a similar sentiment, that the most powerful medicine practitioners have incarnated primarily—or exclusively—in life experiences within the same tribal structure.

I thought of this theory of the ethnic soul when I reflected on a conversation which I had recently with a young friend, a statuesque, blue-eyed, twenty-eight-year-old blonde, whose father I have known since childhood.

"Although I was born into a Scandinavian-Lutheran family in the Midwest," she confided, "I wonder why I have always felt so Jewish. I have always been sympathetic to Jews, and I have always been intrigued by their customs. The very mention of the Holocaust causes my blood pressure to soar with anger. Even my Jewish friends sometimes tease me that I am more Jewish than they are."

Since her father and I had grown up together in the same small prairie town, and I knew the family intimately, I suggested that perhaps her father had never mentioned that, according to family tradition, his great-grandmother had been a Jew.

"Really?" she laughed. "Honest? Daddy never told me that. Well, then, that explains it. It must be genetic memory or something. I'm a non-Jew with a Jewish soul."

I am not decreeing that the young woman had truly discovered the ultimate answer to her troublesome question about her "always feeling so Jewish," but she had found an answer that worked for her. And it may work very well for others. Nowadays, there is a special kind of arrogance that would approach a religious tradition of 5,000 years or more and suggest that its belief concept does not work, because there is a "new age order" that supersedes all previous spiritual philosophies. But I, for one, seek to explore the matter of the ethnic soul a great deal more in my research into past lives.

The Holocaust caused a terrible rent in the psychic fabric of our century. The anguish and terror of more than six million souls cruelly and unjustly torn from life has broadcast into the ethers an anguished chorus of sorrowful, protesting screams that will echo in the minds of sensitive men and women for centuries to come. It is vitally important that people of good will—and perhaps, especially, the young—continue to hear those soulful echoes in order to drown out the foul obscenities issuing from the mouths of the bigoted and the ignorant who proclaim that the Holocaust never happened. May God help us that those who revise history to suit their own sick prejudices will not condemn us to repeat any of the crucial lessons of basic humanity that those who survived the ashes have tried to teach us.

In this wonderful book, Rabbi Gershom and his fourteen fellow storytellers express the kind of unconditional love that can heal the painful soul memories of past lives, the anguish of those who continue to suffer in their present life experiences, and—God willing—the entire planet. I wholeheartedly recommend this book.

Brad Steiger
Author of *Returning from the Light*

Introduction

When it comes to healing, we Jews are very practical people. If a cure works, then we use it, even if we do not fully understand the principles involved. So important are health and healing in Jewish tradition, that the Talmud even permits consulting with a pagan sorcerer, if there is any chance for a cure.[1] Whether we call it religious faith or the placebo effect, the fact remains that healing does sometimes happen through paranormal means.

The people in this book were healed on many levels—physical, emotional, and spiritual—because they believed in reincarnation and psychical phenomena. Whether through dreams and visions, personal meditation, psychic readings or past-life regression therapy, each of these individuals experienced a level of reality beyond the physical world as we know it. Through their encounters with that "other world," they were able to find strength, joy, and inner peace in this world.

The common thread which runs through this collection of testimonials is a karmic connection with the Nazi Holocaust. The majority of the essays were written in response to my previous work, *Beyond the Ashes: Cases of*

Reincarnation from the Holocaust (A.R.E. Press, 1992), which was featured by the Jewish Book Club in 1993 and was a Sponsoring member selection for the Association for Research and Enlightenment (A.R.E.) that same year.

In addition to providing a framework for healing past-life karma, *Beyond the Ashes* also opened a window into the little-known world of Jewish spirituality. For many readers, the idea that Judaism has teachings about reincarnation was more startling than my claim that there were people alive today who "remembered" dying in the Holocaust. Even more amazing, the reincarnation teachings did not come, as one might expect, from the more "progressive" branches of Judaism. Instead, they were preserved—and are still being taught—by the "ultra-orthodox" Hasidim!

A few words of clarification are in order here. Because *Beyond the Ashes* was published by A.R.E. Press, which also publishes works by and about the well-documented American psychic, Edgar Cayce, many readers simply assumed that I must have based my work on the Cayce material, using it to "update" Jewish theology. But the fact is, I was not very familiar with Cayce at the time I wrote *Beyond the Ashes.* The original research was done from a completely Jewish perspective, aimed primarily at people who were already familiar with Hasidic theology. Only later, at the request of the publisher, did I add cross-references from Cayce and other non-Jewish sources in order to make the book accessible to a wider audience.

The resulting balance was highly praised by reviewers in both secular and religious circles. Amy Shapiro wrote in the *Journal of Regression Therapy* that *Beyond the Ashes* fills an important literary void, as it "builds bridges among secular, religious, political, and metaphysical realms" and "guides us through the richness of a language to which few non-Jews are exposed."[2] The *Baltimore Jewish Times*, during a weeklong conference on near-death experiences and reincarnation in 1993, ran a full-page article about my work and that of Dr. Brian Weiss, the Miami psychiatrist who has written extensively on past-life therapy.[3]

Dr. Weiss, who describes himself as "a Reform Jew, I guess," comes from a rationalist Yale Medical School background and originally had no idea that there were Jewish teachings about reincarnation. Today, Hasidic rabbis refer patients to him from around the world. "It's been comforting to me to learn that there are concepts about reincarnation within Judaism that are similar to what I've come to believe on my own," Dr. Weiss explained. "I really thought I was beyond left field with this one until this sort of affirmation started coming in."[4]

If Dr. Weiss was comforted to find his unorthodox psychiatric opinions confirmed by Jewish theology, then I was equally delighted to learn that my Orthodox Jewish beliefs were in accord with the findings of hundreds of past-life therapists! As word about *Beyond the Ashes* continued to spread in therapeutic circles, I was swamped with mail from around the world, describing similar cases and wanting to know, "Where do we go from here?"

Unfortunately, *Beyond the Ashes* did not include many stories about healing. This was because most of the people in that book had talked with me only once or twice, usually during a crisis. In many cases, I was little more than a short rest stop on the long road to recovery. As a result, I ended up with plenty of material about past-life trauma, but virtually no follow-up on healing.

It is my sincere hope that the present volume, *From Ashes to Healing*, will begin to fill this gap. Here you will find personal essays, written by the people themselves, which provide a variety of models for coping with these traumatic memories. From the Nova Scotia goat farmer who dreamed about—and found!—a clock from his previous life to the Jewish artist whose fingers are molding the Holocaust story in clay, each of these individuals was able to work through their inner pain and move "from ashes to healing."

As you read these amazing stories, keep in mind that I am neither a therapist nor a scientist. Prior to becoming known as the "Holocaust reincarnation rabbi," I was simply a storyteller, who told Jewish reincarnation tales from past centuries. Precisely because these classical stories were already in my repertoire, I was not surprised when people came forward with their own past-life memories of dying in the Holocaust. If souls could reincarnate from the Spanish Inquisition in the 1500s or the Chemielnicki Massacres in the 1600s, then why not from Nazi Germany in the twentieth century? At the time, I saw the Holocaust stories as a continuation of this long mystical tradition and interpreted them within a Jewish context, as lost souls on their way back to God.

Once word began to spread that a rabbi was interested in reincarnation, then Gentiles, too, began contacting me about getting "beyond the ashes." They were delighted to have their past-life memories of the Holocaust verified by a Jewish teacher, but I myself was often at a loss about advising them. Although there are well-established Jewish practices for *tikkun* (karmic healing), these don't always translate well across cultures. Without a common vocabulary of symbols and beliefs, I was unable to provide much long-term guidance for non-Jewish seekers. In many cases, although we could agree that reincarnation happens, we did not always agree on how to interpret karma, nor what to do about it.

Much of this disagreement centered around the idea of *yiddishe neshamah* or "Jewish soul." Briefly stated, Jewish mysticism teaches that the souls of the Jews who were present at Mt. Sinai (when the Torah was revealed) will continue to be Jewish for all incarnations, even if they are born into non-Jewish bodies. This idea, so central to Jewish thought, is very different from the more "generic" concepts of the soul as taught by Western metaphysics and many "new age" theologies. Because the idea of "Jewish soul" is so central to my understanding of these stories, I have included an essay which explores this belief from a multicultural perspective. (See Appendix A.)

In addition to stories about "Jewish souls in Gentile bodies," the present volume also contains stories about Jews who came back as Jews once again. In *Beyond the Ashes,* I stated that about two-thirds of the cases were Jewish in their Holocaust lives and have now returned as Gentiles. That certainly was true for the people cited in that book, but, in a much broader context, the "two-thirds" statistic is now completely outdated. Without consciously realizing it, I had failed to take into account a very important cross-cultural factor, which badly skewed the original sample.

In the dominant culture in America, which is based primarily on Protestant Christianity, there is a long tradition of "testifying" about one's personal experiences. Various forms of therapy and twelve-step programs also encourage sharing "I statements" and personal stories in front of the group, while esoteric circles openly discuss their psychic experiences. All of these factors make it relatively easy to collect reincarnation material in the Gentile population.

On the other hand, there is no Jewish model for publicly "testifying" about one's inner life. Quite the contrary.

In Jewish parlance, the greatest saints remain hidden, *their identities known only to themselves and God.* The very idea of standing up in front of the congregation and describing personal dreams and visions is completely alien—and offensive—to the majority of Jews.

Although the secular world has sometimes misunderstood this reticence as "shame-based," the traditional Jewish focus is on *humility,* not shame. Even among the Hasidim, where disciples do openly discuss the greatness of their Rebbes, the Rebbes themselves are expected to modestly deny any miracles attributed directly to them. According to a well-known saying, "The rabbi who must praise himself has a congregation of one." All credit for miracles, Judaism teaches, belongs to God alone.

The practical result of such teachings is that we have very few firsthand records of the spiritual lives of Jews. This does not mean that the spirituality doesn't exist—only that Jews rarely record it for posterity. This lack of Jewish "testimonials" was even noted by the scholar Gershom Scholem, who was reputed to have read every known kabbalistic manuscript in the original languages:

> "In general, it may be said that in the long history of Kabbalism [sic], the number of Kabbalists whose teachings and writings bear the imprint of a strong personality is surprisingly small . . . Among hundreds of Kabbalists whose writings are known to us, hardly ten would provide sufficient material for a biography containing more than a random collection of facts, with little or nothing to give us an insight into their personalities."[5]

Given such strong taboos, where even the greatest

mystics do not commit their personal lives to print, is it any surprise that ordinary Jews were unwilling to tell their stories in a book that linked reincarnation with the Holocaust? No wonder I ended up with stories about Jews who returned as Gentiles!

But now that *Beyond the Ashes* is out, I have been contacted by many, many people who were Jews during the Holocaust and are Jews once again in this life. At this point, I would even venture to say that the *vast majority* of Jewish Holocaust victims have come back as Jews once more. This doesn't negate the material in *Beyond the Ashes* about why some Jews might have returned as Gentiles, but it does suggest that the *percentage* of souls who chose to do this was much, much smaller than the original data implied.

But even if all six million Jews who died in the Holocaust had wanted to come back among their own people, there simply were not enough pregnant Jewish women to provide the bodies. In many cases, according to their own accounts, the returning soul simply grabbed the first available embryo, regardless of race or religion. In other cases, as suggested by Patricia O'Brian in "Keepers of the Joy" (see Chapter Fourteen), there were Jewish souls who consciously chose "voluntary exile" in order to carry out a spiritual mission.

Whatever the reasons, more Jews are coming out of the closet about reincarnation, and my repertoire of "anonymous" stories is much better balanced. At the same time, most Jews are still very reluctant to commit their stories to print. When it came time to collect material for *From Ashes to Healing,* I had plenty of submissions from Gentiles, but found it necessary to specifically seek out Jewish contributors.

In choosing the stories for this book, I tried to include a wide variety of backgrounds, experiences, and beliefs.

If I were a parapsychologist (which I am not), then I probably would have selected only those stories for which hard evidence could be found. But this is not a scientific study. It is an exploration of the human soul, which simply cannot be captured in a test tube. Although some of the stories are corroborated with empirical evidence, others can only offer the healing itself as proof that something extraordinary took place in the lives of these people.

Marcia Hollabaugh (Chapter Six: "More Than a Fairy Tale") and Lena-Marie Broman (Chapter Three: "Flashbacks in Vienna") both did meticulous historical research, attempting to document every detail in their past-life visions. And both found an impressive body of evidence. But for David D. Johnson (Chapter Twelve: "The Scapegoat") and David Moffatt (Chapter Four: "Hands from the Holocaust"), the experience itself was proof enough. In my opinion, both approaches are equally valid when it comes to healing.

Psychiatrist Brian Weiss would probably agree. "Even if you think of it [past-life therapy] as metaphor or as Jungian archetypes," Dr. Weiss explained to the *Baltimore Jewish Times,* "it doesn't seem to matter much when it comes to therapeutic effectiveness. It's actually very much like traditional analysis, except that the arena is enlarged. Instead of stopping at childhood, you go back further in search of trauma that has led to fears, phobias, anxieties, and problematic behavior today."[6]

Because most of the contributors to this book are not professional writers, the reader will no doubt detect my hand in the editing. In some cases, I had to reduce forty or fifty pages of typewritten material to its present form or condense a rambling verbal interview into a concise article. As much as possible, I sought to preserve the flavor of each person's narrative, while keeping in mind the overall content of the book to avoid repetition. Every story was passed back and forth for clarification, and my final version was approved by its author before going to the publisher. Therefore, in spite of my ghost-writing (pun intended), these essays belong to their authors.

Unless otherwise indicated, the footnotes and other supporting material are mine and were added after the essays themselves were finished. It is hoped that the notes will provide the reader with relevant references and, where necessary, further explanations to make the mystical and reincarnation connections clearer. We chose to use this method, rather than incorporate the documentation into the text itself, in order to avoid interrupting the flow of the narratives. In some cases, the writers had already done copious research—complete with sketches, journals, and past-life regression tapes—which they graciously allowed me to use. In other cases, I researched the details myself, much to the delight of the writers, who had no idea how accurate their dreams and visions really were!

There were also instances where I, too, was surprised by the accuracy of the memories. For example, so many people—including three in this book—had claimed to be named "Anna" or "Anna Marie" in their past lives that I wondered if they were subconsciously remembering the well-known story of Anne Frank. In October 1995, I openly raised this very question from the podium. Much to my surprise, Baltimore columnist Sigrid Dreyfus-Manelis, who is also a Holocaust survivor, later told me that "Anna Marie" had been a common name in Europe during the Hitler period. There was, she said, a very popular German song about a girl named "Anna Marie."

My mind immediately flashed back to my own first grade class, where there had been five girls named

"Linda," after an American hit song from my birth year, 1947. Yes, names do go in cycles, which makes the large number of "Annas" seem more plausible.

It goes without saying that the opinions expressed here are those of their authors, and do not necessarily agree with my own views or those of A.R.E. Press. In many cases, especially on the subject of Holocaust karma, they don't even agree with each other.

I regard this diversity of opinion as a very healthy form of dialogue. We are still much too close to the Holocaust to define its "true spiritual meaning," and I, for one, prefer to avoid dogmatic statements—"new age" or otherwise—about Holocaust karma. Because World War II was such an enormous event, involving so many millions of souls on so many different journeys, we could probably find a few cases to "prove" just about any theory imaginable.

Why did the Holocaust happen? There is no single answer, no pat reply that will put it to rest forever. Was it a karmic payback, a divine punishment, a learning experience, a fulfillment of prophecy, a mass martyrdom, or the birth pangs of the Messianic Age? Could all of these explanations have some measure of truth in different cases?

Perhaps the answer lies within the very process of asking the question. Like a Zen koan, "Why the Holocaust?" forces us to examine our own hearts over and over, from all possible angles. Each time we ask the question again, we break through yet another layer of old thought patterns, to confront the world in new ways.

Neti, neti—"not this, not this"—every rational answer is always incomplete. Like the sound of one hand clapping, "Why the Holocaust?" can never be explained in ordinary terms. When all is said and done, the only true reply is the no-answer of silence. In the words of Eli

Wiesel, "Perhaps someday someone will explain how, on the level of man, Auschwitz was possible; but on the level of God, it will remain forever the most disturbing of mysteries."[7]

Reb Yonassan Gershom
Tu B'Shevat, 5756
(The New Year of the Trees)

In the week when we read:
"For I have been a stranger
in a strange land."

Chapter 1:

The Healer Heals Herself

by Abbye Silverstein

I was born Abbye Silverstein on March 10, 1953, to Jewish working-class parents in the Bronx, New York. I grew up in a Jewish home, deeply rooted in Eastern European *Yiddishkeit* (Jewish traditions). My immigrant maternal Russian grandmother lived with us, and she preserved the traditions of Shabbos (the Sabbath) and primary holidays—Rosh Hashanah, Yom Kippur, Hanukkah, and Passover. We observed these holidays by reciting the designated prayers and eating the appropriate foods. I loved Shabbos dinner on Friday nights. The candles, the prayers, the songs, the food—they were all about love.

Every Friday afternoon, in preparation for Shabbos, my grandmother made her ritual sojourn to Allerton Avenue, where she shopped at a combination fish and poultry market. As a preschooler, I went with her to pick out the fish for gefilte fish, and the freshly slaughtered chicken for dinner. I can remember my grandmother sitting in the back of the market, pulling feathers off the chicken and cleaning it to prepare for koshering. She later used these feathers to stuff pillows.

There was something very warm and friendly about all this. On these occasions, it was as if I were being transported in time and place to the Old Country. Yet these happy moments were few and far between. Despite those joys, there was an uncomfortable dichotomy between being Jewish and being American in the post-Holocaust/World War II boom years. What did it mean, I wondered, to be Jewish in America now?

Except for those celebrations around the Shabbos table, my home was an emotional and spiritual desert. This was due to the death of my maternal grandfather just before my birth, and the death of his entire family in Russia during the Holocaust. Because of these recent tragedies, there was no warmth on a daily basis in our house; our communications concerned everyday routine functions. My family was unconsciously mourning, but how could a child know that? I would reach out to hug my parents and grandmother and they would appease me—sometimes. It was as if everyone lived in his or her own separate rooms, not wanting to be disturbed. I felt like I didn't belong to this family, like a stranger in a strange land, and I longed for *my own* family . . . So I found my solace by meditating and praying.

My Hebrew school teacher, who had survived the camps, made me feel cold, empty, and dead inside. Was it her? Or was it me? Or was she simply a mirror for my higher self, triggering a flashback to something that my conscious ego would not allow me to fully remember?

At the age of seven, I watched my first Holocaust documentary on PBS and cried uncontrollably. My mother joked about this, saying that I cried as if I had been there. But to me, it was no joke. In my mind, a voice answered, "Yes, I was there."

Plus, there were other flashbacks or "bleed-throughs" that I couldn't explain. I was deeply disturbed by the sight of a Mercedes-Benz dealership on Boston Post Road and would be filled with fear when riding in a fast car on winding roads. Sometimes this fear would cause me to go into a numbed, speechless trance. In my child's mind, I thought it was just my active imagination that took me into this "other world," which held a wide range of emotions for me—happy, loving, scared, confused. So I took bits and pieces of those memories and converted them into present-day scenarios, combining both lifetimes into one, in an attempt to fill the emptiness in my present life.

I would often flash back on a dark-haired, bearded man, feeling as if he had had a great love affair with me. For many years in this life, I searched for him in every male-female relationship that I had. I longed for his love, his presence, his mind, and his heart. It was not until he later appeared to me on the astral plane that I finally found him again in this life.

At the age of thirteen, I was diagnosed with scoliosis, a curvature of the spine. The spine is the backbone of the body, providing structure and support—the container for the central nervous system to send messages to all parts of the body. So why was my spine twisted and deformed into an S-curve? Was it merely physiological? Or was it spiritual and emotional, too?

At the age of twenty, while I was in college, I had an abortion. After the abortion, I went home to rest and had a puzzling dream:

> I was dressed in 1930s garb, walking away from a college campus filled with Gothic-style buildings. I turned back toward the campus, looked at one particular building with large stained-glass windows,

and said goodbye for the last time. Then I walked toward a black Mercedes-Benz with a dark-haired, bearded man in the driver's seat. Again, I looked back to say goodbye. We drove away, and the word DEATH appeared before me.

I awoke feeling very disturbed. But I would not understand this dream until much later, when my first past-life regression revealed the memories that I had stored within my higher self.

All my life, I have instinctively believed in past lives and was drawn to "new age" ideas and mysticism, especially kabbalah. But I also felt disjointed, always searching, never at ease . . . By the fall of 1978, I had hit rock bottom. It was time to end my marriage, and this was both liberating and frightening. Here I was, a twenty-five-year-old hippie without any real financial security and with a child to support. The idea of being a single mother was overwhelming, but choosing to remain in a chemically dependent marriage would have been more damaging to myself and my year-old son. In desperation, I began to pray three times a day to G-d[1] for help.

On the weekend of December 1–3, 1978, my prayers were answered with a series of psychic dreams. The final dream revealed the initial clue which led to my first past-life regression:

A dark-haired, bearded man appeared to me, dressed in modern-day clothing. He identified himself as Richard [pronounced as in German: ree-KHARD) and gave me this message: "You and I were lovers. We were married in a past life and died together. We have come back to be together again, to continue the work we started. It will be soon."

I realized that the man in this dream was the same dark-haired man I had been dreaming about all my life! But over the next few months, my focus was on more earthly concerns: my separation, divorce, and getting my life in order. Then one day in July 1979, I came home from work to meditate, and, while meditating, I met the astral projection of the dark-haired man from my dream in December. I had mixed feelings about this meeting. My ego was shocked and angry that he had invaded my space, while my higher self was delighted to be reunited with him once more.

At the same time, I thought for sure that I must be going crazy, so I confided in some friends who were well-versed in psychic phenomena. They all agreed that I needed to have a past-life regression, because I had "unfinished business" with this man from my last incarnation. Two days later, I was hypnotized by a professional who specialized in this type of work. The story which I now share emerged in stages, through a series of regression sessions. Putting the pieces together has helped me understand the "bleed-throughs" between my current and past lives.

* * *

In my Holocaust life, I was Anna, a German Jewish woman who grew up in the working-class section of Berlin with her mother, father, and younger sister. We were a close-knit, traditional family, with much love and warmth. Shabbos was celebrated weekly by the entire clan—grandparents, uncles, aunts, and cousins—who ate, prayed, and sang together.

Anna was very pretty, yet she viewed her physical beauty as secondary to her intellectual prowess. She aspired to become a psychiatrist and attended the University of Heidelberg where she met her husband, Richard. He had been raised in an upper-class, Reform Jewish family, who did not approve of Anna. But Richard married her anyway, against his father's wishes. Anna and Richard were true soul mates, perfectly matched physically, emotionally, mentally, and spiritually. Nothing could keep them apart.

At the university, they shared the same passion and purpose in life—to raise consciousness and improve humanity. He was driven by politics and law, and she by psychology and medicine. Caught up in the history of their time, Richard became involved in a student dissident group on campus.[2]

In the spring of 1933, Anna had a miscarriage, and Hitler won the election. The Brown Shirts were now after the dissidents. Richard insisted that he and Anna should leave the country and go to England for safety, because many of their friends had already been beaten up and harassed. So Anna closed their affairs with the university and packed their belongings to escape to England.

As they drove through the forest enroute to France, Richard became enraged at the ignorance of the German people for believing in Hitler. He was also angry about his own father's denial of the political situation and the loss of his friends, his dreams, and his future. Richard seemed out of control, and Anna was frightened and helpless. She begged him to slow down as he drove at breakneck speed on the winding roads in the dark forest. There was a long stretch of silence between them. Suddenly, at a curve in the road directly ahead of the car, they saw a large, imposing tree . . .

The next thing Anna knew, her spirit had left her body, and she was dead. So was Richard. They stood there together in the spirit, viewing their own corpses. The car had crashed into a tree, and Richard's chest had been crushed against the steering wheel. Anna had fallen forward into the windshield.

Anna exclaimed, "We're *dead!* We're *dead!* Only the body dies. Consciousness never dies! Consciousness lives forever!" Then she looked at Richard and asked, "Why did you do this?"

Solemnly he replied, "I had a vision. I heard a voice telling me to come with them. That they would save us. Then I saw soldiers coming to take us away. We were separated by barbed wire. I knew that one of us would live and the other would die. I couldn't bear to be separated from you . . . and the next thing I saw was the tree. I couldn't stop the car soon enough. Anna, please forgive me. But it is better to die by the hands of love than by the hands of hate."

Anna forgave Richard. They remained earthbound in the German countryside and met other discarnate spirits who were also in limbo like themselves. One day, they saw soldiers (still in the flesh) marching on the road and heard gunshots in the distance. They went to investigate and found the bodies of dead Jews in a large open pit or grave. Anna screamed, "They're killing us! They're killing the Jews! Richard, you were right—you saved us!"

Of course, he had not saved them from death. But he had saved them from the horrible humiliation of being tortured by the Nazis just because they were Jews. Richard replied, "Anna, now you understand that it is better to die by the hands of love than by the hands of hate." At that moment, they heard a Voice calling to them. The time had come to transcend the earth plane. White-golden light appeared, showing them the way to the in-between life.

In the spirit world, they were welcomed by a guard standing beside a large door. He walked them to a reception table in the Great Hall. A woman there welcomed them and explained that they were going to continue their lives in this world now. She told them that they were in training to help others. They had been spared the horrors of the Holocaust in order to be of service to the victims. They were sent to heavenly classes, where they studied with the great Jewish masters about religion, philosophy, psychology, and the psychic healing of the soul.

Anna's first assignment in the spirit world was as an intake worker. On the earth below, the Jews were being exterminated, and souls were entering the in-between world at a very rapid rate. She was placed in the Great Hall, which was like the "Ellis Island" of Heaven, run by the "United Jewish Appeal" of the in-between world.[3] The Jewish souls came in droves, with their astral bodies crippled and mangled with torture, degraded, and stripped of their dignity.

As an intake worker, Anna took their vital statistics for the Akashic Record: name, place of birth, residence, occupation, family history, manner of death, etc. Soon she met her mother, father, sister, and best friend as they stood in line to check in. They had died in the Holocaust. Like the rest of the Jews, they were sent to a section of the afterworld that was designated "for Jews only"—not to segregate them, but to provide a place where their wounded spirits could heal in an atmosphere of safety.[4]

This Jewish part of Heaven was divided into countries, cities, villages, and towns, which paralleled their homes on earth. Bulletin boards were created according to geographical regions, which posted messages for the incoming souls to find their relatives. Maps and signposts aided them in going home. Everything that had been left behind on the material plane was re-created in the spirit world in order to help these severely wounded souls make the transition toward reincarnating as the Baby Boom generation. There was a great deal of work to do in a very short period of time.

Anna was happy in the in-between world, and her life was very productive. She was "promoted" several times, until she was the supervisor of a type of healing center. As such, she attended a council of healing center administrators, to share ideas for healing and helping these Holocaust souls make the transition.

When the war ended in 1945, the Jewish section was opened up, and people were able to travel to other parts of the in-between world. Anna's husband, Richard, was preparing to reincarnate again, to be among the first wave of Baby Boomers. Anna, on the other hand, did not want to leave. Richard promised that they would find each other someday, then bid her goodbye. Anna grieved the loss of her husband, but felt content to remain in the in-between world. She realized that life is a continuum and she did not want to accept the restrictions of a physical body.

Nevertheless, by 1950 Anna could not hold out any longer. The time had come for her to be reincarnated again, but her designated mother had a miscarriage. Anna was relieved, because she wasn't ready to return yet. Three years later, she was told that she would have to enter the womb and attach to the embryo at the moment of conception, rather than wait until birth, because her mother had a fibroid tumor. By entering the womb at conception, Anna would ensure that the fetus survived to become her new body.

Reluctantly, Anna agreed. With the help of her two spirit guides, Ruth and Isaac, she wrote the contract for her new life on earth. The first forty years would be filled with struggle, physical and emotional pain, mental and spiritual challenges, learning, and the repaying of karmic debt. After this period, she would prosper materially and be able to serve G-d as a healer once more. Her guides promised that they would remain active in her life, providing the opening for her to remain connected to the spiritual worlds.

Anna then entered the dark womb, but stayed in a meditative trance, connected to the spirit world by a ray of white light. She remained in this meditative state until her birth on March 10, 1953, at 3:25 A.M. At that moment, the ray of light was severed, and Anna was born into the material world as Abbye Silverstein.

* * *

As Abbye, I spent over a decade consciously mourning and grieving the losses of Anna's life. I struggled to complete her goals and was met with obstacle after obstacle. Finally, I took control of my own life in this incarnation, for myself and for my son. I stopped grieving. I forgave myself and laid Anna's driven memories to rest. I kept my love for Richard on the soul level, but let go of my yearning for him in this life.

I decided to pursue a career in counseling and acupuncture, in order to continue being a healer in this present life. It was through my study and practice of these healing arts that my own physical, mental, and spiritual pain was also healed, enabling me to release the sorrow of Anna and the Holocaust.

On two occasions, as part of this healing process, I visited the United States Holocaust Memorial Museum in Washington, D.C. The first visit was a major healing process, which enabled me to let go of the pain, suffering, and victimization that Anna had taken on when she was healing the Jewish souls in the in-between world. Although I had been spared the degradation of a horrible death as Anna, the sorrow of the victims had become mine in this life as Abbye. Due to the scoliosis, my body had even become crippled and mangled like their astral bodies. At the museum, I finally released that sorrow. I also forgave Richard for taking Anna's life without consulting her and prayed that he could forgive himself for the guilt which drove him to come to me in my dreams.

In the spring of 1995, I visited the museum again. This time, I went as an observer, not a participant. The museum itself now holds the painful emotions that I had carried for forty years, thus freeing me to let go of the sorrow. It is also the beginning of the healing process for the Jewish community and for the world. Now that the museum bears witness, those six million souls can move on.

The joy of being free of my past-life baggage is a gift from G-d, which I now cherish every day. Sometimes I still struggle with the question of how to be Jewish in America, and I long for the closeness that I knew in the in-between world. But at the same time, I also remember why I am here. The Jewish community on earth is only now beginning to heal from the trauma of the Holocaust. And in my heart and soul, I know that I came back to help with that healing, to help create a renewed and joyous Judaism for the present and future generations.

Chapter 2:

The Clock

by Bruce Whittier

My story begins in the spring of 1991. According to my dream journal for April 8 of that year, I began having very vivid dreams about the Second World War. The dreams continued to come for nearly two weeks. This is what I dreamed:

> I found myself living in a foreign country with a wife, a daughter and son, and an older man. We also had a black and white dog.
>
> It was wartime and I was afraid, having been warned that the Germans were going to invade the Netherlands. As Dutch Jews living in Holland, our lives were in danger, because of something I had learned while working in my office. The details of this information are not clear, but I think it had something to do with politics.
>
> In the basement of our house was an old root cellar, where we decided to find shelter. The room was cold and dark, but it was a safe hideout. Against one

> wall, we had put a square table, with a clock sitting on it, so that we could keep track of the time. The chime of the clock was gentle and quiet.
>
> One day, I had crawled through the opening to our hideout in order to take the dog outside. It was very early in the morning—dawn had just broken—and there was mist or fog in the air. As I entered the backyard, everything was still, but the dog began to sense something.
>
> Before I knew it, somebody was speaking to me and accusing me of some crime. At first I resisted arrest, but they shot the dog and then threatened me.

When I awoke from this dream, I was very shaken up. I wondered and worried about it all day, asking myself what it could possibly mean. The next night I had the same dream, and again the night after that. On the third night, I was told that the clock was now here in Canada. I thought to myself, what an imagination! But the dream actually gave specific directions: Travel on Route 1 [in Nova Scotia], and there will be a new antique shop. The clock is there.

I put this trip off for several weeks, but the dreams continued, giving me more details:

> We were at a camp of some sort—we have been told it is Auschwitz—and I can still smell chicken cooking. Ashes and dust covered everything. Parts of this are sketchy and not very clear, but I remember my wife and I being summoned. We were taken to an area where there was a large trench. We couldn't see what was in there until we were made to stand at the edge. It was a mass grave. Here we were shot. I took a bullet through the heart area. I

can still see the bodies in the trench.

As I wrote this, the tears filled my eyes and my emotions ran rampant. Why, I asked myself—Why? First of all, I am not Jewish, and secondly, I am only twenty-nine years old—so why was I dreaming about things which happened fifty years ago? How could I be remembering a war that was over before I was even born?

In this life, my contact with Jews has been almost nonexistent. I have met only two that I am aware of, and talking on the phone to Rabbi Gershom about this story makes a third. In the little Canadian town of 1,600 people where I grew up, there are no Jews. Nor do I have any Jewish ancestors that I am aware of. Our family originally came from England in the 1700s. We are just ordinary folks who work hard and love life. So why would I, a Canadian goat farmer, be dreaming about Dutch Jews in the Holocaust?

Finally, I decided to take the venture and look for the antique store. But I didn't want to go alone, so I asked a close friend to travel with me. And sure enough, there was a new antique shop on Route 1. The shop was called "In Tyme"—a strange archaic spelling, but how appropriate! We drove up to the parking lot and ventured into the store.

There were lots of nice antique pieces, but no clock.

Oh well, I thought to myself, it was just a silly dream. We were about to leave, when the antique dealer came out from the back room to greet us. He closed the door behind him—and there, hidden from our sight when the door had been open, *was the very same clock from my dream!* I was not only stunned, I was in shock. That clock was mine, or at least it had been in another life.

Of course, I wasn't about to tell a complete stranger that I had dreamed about owning his clock in another incarnation—what would he think? Still, I wanted to know more about its history. So I asked the shopkeeper where he had picked up such lovely pieces. He began telling me how he had just returned from Europe, where he had purchased many different pieces. He had found a lot of them in Holland, where the authorities had opened up some old warehouses full of unclaimed possessions from Dutch Jews during World War II—beautiful things which had been confiscated by the Nazis. This clock had been among those Jewish pieces.

This was just too much of a coincidence! I wanted to touch the clock, to hold it in my hands and see if I could get any psychic feelings from it. But it was very expensive, and I could not afford it, so I didn't have any plausible excuse to handle it. I left the shop without actually touching the clock, but was glad to know that it really did exist.

All of this remained in my mind on a daily basis—the first thing when I woke up and the last thing before retiring for the evening. As I sat quietly and looked back over my life, I could clearly see how there had been other incidents, puzzling at the time, which now seemed connected to that same life as a Dutch Jew.

The first of these happened when I was nine or ten years old. My parents were watching a war movie, and I began to panic. I do not know exactly which movie it was, but I clearly remember being sent to my room and not being allowed to watch television that night.

Later, as a young teenager, we moved several streets away to an old house that was built by a sea captain around 1870. I distinctly remember that I was about fourteen at the time. My mother, grandmother, a couple of friends, and I had gone shopping at a secondhand clothing store. While going through a bin full of odds and ends, I discovered two Jewish scullcaps and immediately bought them. One was brown velvet and the other was multicolored silk. Each day after school, I would wear one of these while I was studying. It made me feel like I belonged. And another strange thing—all my life, I have never liked pork, and only on rare occasions will I eat it. I find this meat offensive, and it has a terrible taste to me.

But why should I have these Jewish ideas at all? I was raised in the United Church of Canada and later joined the Pentacostal movement, where belief in reincarnation at any level is unheard of. So I certainly did not get this from my upbringing! In 1982, I had a genuine experience of being baptized in the Holy Spirit, including speaking in tongues. This was a wonderful experience, and since that time, I have spoken in another language, which one person told me was Yiddish, whatever that is.[1] Now I began to wonder. Could this, too, be past-life related?

* * *

In August 1995, after talking with Rabbi Gershom, I decided to undergo hypnotic regression in order to get to the bottom of all this. The hypnotist was George McAdoo, who conducts reincarnation seminars here in Nova Scotia.[2] Under hypnosis, I saw myself as a Dutch Jew named Stefan Horwitz,[3] who was married to a woman named Helene. They had two children. The clock was there, too. It was a family heirloom which had belonged to my grandmother in that life. Under hypnosis, I could see it on the little table in my parents' sitting room and hear its soft chime. When the Nazis came, we took it with us into our hiding place.

Many sketchy details in the dream were now filled in. The hiding place was not in a basement as I had previously thought. It was a root cellar at my grandfather's place. There was a small space we could get into down there, that we planned to conceal with bags of dirt and potatoes. I even remembered how Helene had sewed straps to the backs of the potato sacks, so that we could pull them in behind us to block the entrance to the secret bunker.

As the Nazis were nearing our village, Papa gave me the clock and told me to go, to take it to the underground bunker and hide with Helene, Grampa, and the children, charging me to look after them. He and Mama would stay at their own place.

The Germans came. We entered the bunker. As in the dream, I went outside in the early morning with our little dog. But under hypnosis, more details were now revealed.

After the German soldier shot the dog, he took me inside the house and beat me until I broke down and revealed the location of the hiding place. Grampa, Helene, the children, and I were then arrested and taken away in a truck. For several months we were interred in some kind of ghetto, where we had to barter for food. I remember giving one man my hat for half a loaf of bread. Eventually we were loaded into trucks again.

> [Under hypnosis:] We are going to a place where the trains are. We are unloaded, we give them our names—Stefan and Helene Horwitz—and they say, "Over there! All of you, go there!" So we go into this car where there are many others. It smells awful. It's hard to catch a good breath of air. They close the door, but we are all together. And the train starts and goes . . .
>
> It's been several days and we have nothing to eat yet. We are cold and hungry. The train keeps going.

You start to lose the sense of time and how long. Now we are in another country. They say that this is a camp. [Are you still in the train?] Yes, but the train is coming to the camp. It is pulling up . . .

Each car is unloaded, one by one, and people are pushed and shoved and told to go. We are unloaded, and it is nice to finally breathe the air . . . We are walking now towards a station and they stop to ask us our names and they say that the children must go this way, and Helene says, "NO! I want my children!" And they say, "No, the children must go." Grampa is still behind, but he is very weak and very old . . .

Helene and I are sent to a place and separated. I enter . . . I have to take off my clothes. They say that I am a dirty Jew, and to sit . . . and they shave my hair—it feels awful, falling and hitting my shoulders. I say to myself, why must I do this? They then pass me some clothes. These aren't my clothes . . . "These are your new clothes here . . . " They send me to a place with many bunks. There are other people. Their heads are shaven. They look hungry, but they still have a spirit about them. Trust in our God . . . [Bruce shivers] It's cold in here . . .

Today, there is a funny odor on the air—it reminds me of Mama cooking the chicken. It helps soothe the hunger in my stomach. I ask *what is that?* And they all stare at me. One man says, "You do not know? That is the smell of the dead people. They must dispose, they say, so that we all don't get sick and die." It looks almost like snow out, but it is like a dust. I put my hand out, and it's dusty . . .

[McAdoo: How long are you there?] About six or seven months.

. . . Now it's spring. It's actually warm, and I'm

> cold. They call me "Jew." Here there are several of us. And they bring Helene. I see the men on horses, their leather boots and their nice saddles. There must be two dozen of us. They make us walk and walk. They take us out through a gate, with the horses alongside of us. You can feel the people staring and watching. My clothes are so big, I have to keep hauling them up. I'm not allowed to touch Helene. And they keep walking us. We see behind us, in the glimpse of our eye, the camp . . .
>
> We come to a place where there is a trench, but I can't see into the trench. There are people in front of us and they are being shot and pushed into the trench and they fall. [Bruce gasps, inhales sharply.] I know what is going to happen . . . I see people, there's so many people in the trench. Some are still moving [breathes heavily]. Then all of a sudden I feel it—like a hot knife going through me. And they shoot me through the back and I fall. [Takes a deep breath.] I'm not dead yet. I have others fall . . . on top . . . of me. They're getting so heavy . . . I can't breathe.

At this point in the session, my breathing became very labored, and I began to shiver and sob in fear. You can actually hear it on the tape—it really was hard for me to breathe, as if I were reliving it all over again. George McAdoo, the hypnotist, intervened with suggestions to "let go of the physical." He then asked me where I was in relation to my body from that life. At that point, the whole scene changed into a vision of light:

> I am above . . . floating in white light . . . Helene . . . our hands are outreached. It is like a peace after such a long time . . . Grampa is reaching down, tell-

ing us come this way, come this way . . . and we are floating in a bubble, safe. What's happened below is so far away now . . .

It is like we are going through a wall, but it's clear and I am very thin. It's like the bubble is going up through it and—it just opens! And here is a place, you hear the laughter and you hear music. There's lots of blue color, but it seems so *big,* like a *massive* big hall. It's a place of such peace and quiet . . . [surprised]—I'm not hungry!

It's like floating, just floating down or straight ahead . . . There are just people everywhere, and a bright light. The light is so bright, away in the distance. There are so many people, some waiting to go, some just arriving like us. The light is so bright—it's warm, it feels so nice . . . it's so intense. People are going into it, they're just blending into it, but you can hear them, like children on a school field playing and laughing.

We are getting closer to the light. A-h-h-h, it just feels so good to enter into it, it's like a kaleidoscope of white lights, and you're just floating and you're just there . . . it's all feeling, it's not so much sight, it's feeling.

I hear trumpets and horns, but there's a deep, deep blue light.[4] As the horns play, I hear them just calling, it's a sound of calling . . . and everybody is drawn into the light, into the sounds, very deep into the light . . .

[McAdoo: Is it your time?] It's everybody's time. Everybody's being drawn at the same time, just deeper into the light, towards this sapphire blue color . . . There's a massive flame, and it's in the distance, but it's so bright you can't look, it radiates out from it—so intense, so pure looking. And the trumpets and horns are still blowing . . . There's a voice, a large voice coming forward, saying, "You are now here. Here you are now. Be forever, light eternal." The voice just goes. We feel in awe. No one is saying anything. You don't see anything . . . you are just here now. It's like you need not say anything . . . There's now a waiting place, a time to examine what you've learned and how you've grown.

[McAdoo: Why did you choose to live in that part of the twentieth century?] I was *sent* there. To obtain a higher level of peace. To gain strength and knowledge, to grow, to be able to teach and to guide others.

[McAdoo: Did you accomplish all of those lessons?] Yes.

After that magnificent vision of the afterlife, I was finally able to let go of the pain and fear from the Holocaust memories. And the clock? It's still for sale, at a different store in another province. They are holding it for me until I can afford to buy it. It's amazing to see that after four years it still has not been sold, as if it is waiting for me to come and finally take it home.

(EPILOGUE: The clock itself is an expensive antique, beyond the family budget of the Whittiers. When Rabbi Gershom told this story from place to place, many people donated to the "ransom the clock fund" in order to help return the clock to Bruce and be a part of this amazing past-life story. In May 1996, the clock was finally redeemed from its long exile and brought to the Whittier home, where it now sits in a place of honor.

Chapter 3:

Flashbacks in Vienna

by Lena-Marie Broman

The phoenix bird rises from the ashes . . . This is the picture I carry in my mind of my way to healing, of how I became the person I am today—sometimes slowly, sometimes quickly, but, in the end, sparkling with colors and with great strength inside.

I've had my Holocaust past-life memories more or less all my life. As a child, I played that I was a Jew, making some kind of Jewish bread and doing other Jewish ceremonies. These were *not* things I could have known anything about at the age of five, growing up as a nonpracticing Christian in Sweden!

Later, when I was in school, I was confronted with some of the horrifying movies from the Auschwitz concentration camp. I nearly fainted. My teacher pulled me out of the classroom, trying to talk with me, and I remember how he got very frightened, because of my strong feelings about the Second World War.

And I spoke about Vienna! How much I wanted to go there, and how I longed for that town, even though I had never seen Vienna in this life. Deep inside, I felt that I had really lost someone and something, but I couldn't remember exactly who or what. Not until 1993 did I have the opportunity to visit "my" Vienna again, and it was like coming home! Later in this article, I will tell you further details about that trip. But first, let me share some more of the Holocaust memories that came to me and what I did to accept them, to make them a part of my life today.

In 1979, I was vacationing on Tenerife, an island off the Atlantic coast of Africa, with my mother and three other relatives. We went into a German cafe somewhere in the southern part of the island. I felt a terrible foreboding when I heard German marching music coming through the big loud speakers outside the cafe—music that I somehow knew very well. Of course, they were only playing this for the beer garden atmosphere, but hearing that music felt terrible to me, and I began to feel cold in the warm sunshine.

Suddenly, I noticed an elderly blond woman, about seventy years old, standing in the open doorway. She was looking straight at me, and my intuitive feelings about her were just terrible! She didn't move her eyes one bit. She just continued staring at me, and her eyes were cold and icy.

Inside of myself, the scene before my own eyes suddenly shifted, and I "saw" her standing behind a wire fence, as a female guard in a Nazi concentration camp. I knew beyond a doubt she had been there—and I knew that we had met before![1]

I wanted to run, but since I was with four other people,

we entered and took a table in the cafe. I tried to calm down. But all this time, that old German woman kept staring right into my eyes with that cold, bone-chilling grimness. Suddenly I just couldn't stand it anymore. I panicked. Leaving the coffee and cake on the table, I ran out the door of the cafe and into some shops farther away, to escape from that old woman's icy stare.

Later on, my traveling companions and I talked about what had happened. My mother suggested that maybe it is possible that we are living more lives than one. At that time, however, I pushed it all away, and my daily life went on. I never doubted that these memories of another life were real. But, there were so many other things going on in my life *now,* that I couldn't—or maybe it just wasn't the right time—bring myself to work with it seriously.

During those years, I also had a very big personal problem. I think it started when I was around twelve years old, and it got steadily worse. I felt frightened among other people, even though I liked people. For some unknown reason, I also developed a strange phobia. I was afraid of vomiting in the streets, irrationally feeling that, if I ever did vomit, then the police would arrest me. During the 1980s, when I was working as a guide for a Swedish travel company, I had to confront these ridiculous fears every morning, when I would go to meet the busload of tourists. I hated myself for being so weak that I simply could not enjoy life.

And then, there were the dreams. Horrifying nightmares about dogs—big and black—with wire fences and soldiers. Still, I refused to see what it was really all about. But it was impossible to suppress it, and I was confronted with my past life more and more.

In 1989, the "big thing" happened which really made me aware of the truth about my two intertwined lives.

My former husband and I were traveling by car in the west coast of Sweden. Because I grew up on the east coast of Sweden, I had never been to this area before. By "chance" we found ourselves driving along a small road, among hills and green trees, when something strange began to happen to me. It was as if the skies were closing in, while feelings of deep despair and grief rose up inside me.

I started to pray and asked my husband to slow down the car, because I was sure that something terrible was about to happen to us—maybe a car accident or worse. My husband looked at me, very confused, but he also knew that I could intuitively see and feel things that he could not. So, he took my request seriously and slowed down.

A few minutes later, I blurted out, "There it is!"

"What is?" my husband asked, staring at me.

I pointed to my right. There was a military camp, rather broken down, behind a big wire fence. We stopped the car just outside the fence, and my husband asked if we should backtrack along the road and try to find out why I had reacted so strangely. "Yes," I said. My heart was still beating so rapidly, and I could still feel that heavy sorrow.

We drove back some meters, and, suddenly, everything was dark all around me. My legs ached, and my left cheek felt like a big wound. I knew then that I had lost my entire family in the other life. I "saw" my two children, and I "saw" myself arriving at this camp in one of the Red Cross buses, weak and without hope.[2] I knew then that I had died in another life.

I couldn't take it anymore. Desperately, I shouted to my husband to drive on, *right now!* So he did. About a hundred meters later, I felt like "myself" again. I then took a small compact out of my handbag, to look at my face in the mirror after all of that crying. *There, on my left cheek, was a big white scar—something that had never been there before!*

We stopped the car again. My husband looked at my cheek, shaking his head and muttering something about "strange things," but he could not doubt what he saw with his own eyes. We went straight back to the hotel, and he took a photograph of my cheek. It was not until late in the evening that the mysterious scar finally faded away, and my cheek was normal again.

For three weeks after that, I woke up every night screaming, with nightmares of bombs falling, my frightened children, and how I was kept in a concentration camp as a prisoner . . . I was terrified, and my poor husband did not understand what was happening. How could he? But for me, it was like a curtain had been raised, and I realized that I had, indeed, lived a life before.

Actually, I had been remembering parts of it all my life, so these mental pictures were, in one way, natural for me. But, in another way, they were not so natural at all. This placed a strain on our relationship, and, in 1990, my husband and I divorced.

That same year, my grandmother, who was like a mother to me, also died suddenly. This, on top of the Holocaust memories and the divorce, made things even worse. I felt totally alone and very, very sad. My feelings of fear became increasingly worse. I had great difficulty going out into the streets; even a trip to the post office became a nightmare. I realized that I had reached the end of my rope, and that I *had* to find out more about my past life. What had really happened to me back then?

So, I contacted a psychotherapist in Stockholm who utilized hypnosis as a treatment, which I thought would be excellent for me to try. I had found his address in a book by Dr. Raymond Moody, which had been translated by a close friend of the therapist—a point which later played a big part in this unfolding story.

Yes, more strange things continued to happen. The moment I looked into the eyes of the Stockholm therapist, I recognized him! I knew immediately that he had been part of my past life, but, at the time, I didn't know how. I felt perfectly safe with him, but, at the same time, I also felt that big sadness overwhelming me again.

Previously, I had thought that I might have been a prisoner at the Dachau concentration camp, because it was near Austria, which had been my homeland in the other life. Under hypnosis, however, I learned that I had really been in the Buchenwald camp, which was in eastern Germany. I also found out more about my family life in that other incarnation. I had had two children by a German husband, who was a Nazi officer. Most of this I had already suspected or "knew" intuitively, but I still wanted it confirmed somehow.

Then, still under hypnosis, I suddenly saw Carl—the hypnotherapist conducting the session—as one of the soldiers in the camp, as one of the Nazi officers. I later told him about this, and he seemed to accept it all. He didn't recognize me in that way [i.e., as someone he knew from another life], but he felt something very strong, something—I think—more than love.

Some months after the treatment was over, he called me, and we started to meet as friends. There were many strong feelings between us, which deepened into a warm friendship. I was feeling much better now. I had found out a lot about my life and death in the camp, and was able to get on with my life, knowing that, when the right moment came, I would be brave enough to dig deeper into those memories.

One autumn evening, I met a very special man. He

turned out to be the translator of the book by Raymond Moody, in which I had first found the address of Carl, my former therapist! This new acquaintance and I soon fell in love, and I found myself living with him. "Somewhere between heaven and hell"—that's how I prefer to describe our year together.

During one of the first evenings we spent together, he put on a phonograph record, and the room was filled with the music of Bach. Not the heavy stuff that I had heard before, but a small chorale, which affected me deeply. In fact, I went straight into a trance!

Psychic pictures of the past life totally overwhelmed me, and they were as clear as my childhood memories are today. I saw my husband in that life, playing the piano, and I knew that his favorite song was that same chorale by Bach. I could see his appearance in detail: his warm, glittering smile, his curly blond hair, and those clear blue eyes. His name was Jürg.

I also saw my two children from that life, Naima and Heinz. Naima was the oldest, with beautiful eyes and a lovely personality. Heinz was two years younger than his sister Naima and was a very serious young man. He was born in 1939, some months before the war started. I remember that I had difficulties really loving him, because he was not "allowed" to be born, but I ignored that order from the Nazis.[3]

Also during that strange evening, with all of my memories "floating" before my eyes, I "saw" the years I'd spent in Vienna, before the concentration camp. In that life, I had been Anna-Maria Kellerman, a young Jewish woman from an assimilated Viennese family.

Some months later, all the memories became clear to me about what had happened in Buchenwald. Carl—my former therapist and good friend in this life—had been the commandant of the camp! It was he who had given me the scar on my cheek, which had so strangely reappeared then faded again in this life. This psychic revelation also explained a great deal about our current relationship and the pain and sadness which I connected with him.

In the Buchenwald camp, I had been his mistress. He was very abusive, even forcing me to get on my knees and beg for my life. At the same time, he also loved me deeply, even though I was a Jew. When I "remembered" the story, I could also feel the love and the hopelessness all over again—how he had tried to save me in 1944, begging me to leave the camp. He had one chance to get me out of there, but I refused to leave. I had nothing left in the world but him. All of my family was gone, my parents taken by the Nazis in 1941, my children separated from me in the railway station after the arrest, and my husband killed just before that. Why should I leave the only person in my life that I could now trust a little bit, even if he was abusive, even if my life was in danger? Some weeks later, he, too, was killed, and I was left completely alone in the world.

All of those pictures and feelings were rushing through me during 1992-'93, and I let myself feel everything. For the first time in my life—this one—I stopped struggling against the memories. The time had come for me to be brave.

In the summer of 1993, I traveled with my good friend, Dr. Göran Grip,[4] to Buchenwald, in what was formerly East Germany. There, I was physically confronted with the sight of the camp once again. In a way, I became healed by those very things and circumstances that happened on our journey to this place.

By "chance," we arrived at the town of Buchenwald very late in the evening, and we drove up the hill to see if there was a place to sleep close to the camp. Everything was closed and dark, and Göran wanted to return to Weimar for the night. I insisted that we should go on, and so we did.

Suddenly I spotted some lights on my right and suggested to Göran that we should drive there. With some resistance, he did, and we went to inquire about renting a room. To make a long story short, we ended up spending the night in a house that had once belonged to the SS! (Technically, we were not allowed to stay there at all. It was inside the actual site of the camp, and, although there were rooms, these were reserved for archaeological students from Berlin.)

Of course, I was terrified during the long, dark hours of the night. But when the morning arrived and the sun was shining so brightly, I felt healed. The lady in charge, Frau Billig, prepared a beautiful breakfast, just for Göran and me, which she served to us privately in a special room. Frau Billig was so gracious and understanding, giving us so much that she didn't need to give, as if, on some level, she had sensed the importance of our visit there.

Before this journey—which was really a kind of spiritual quest—I had described the camp, including the small, gray house of the commandant.[5] Now here it was, exactly as I had remembered it. Oh yes, it was so hard for me, but still—I could feel the wounds in my spirit being healed.

Then it was on to Vienna, "my" town. When we got there, I opened the window and took it all in. The feeling, and especially the smell. That is a very special thing in Vienna. You can still smell a strange mix of horse manure, lavender soap, and coffee, which I remembered so clearly from my past life.

We arrived at the Vienna hotel around noon and went out to look for all those places that I had already described while still back in Sweden: my apartment, my father's shop, my favorite cafe.[6] At first we used a map, but after a few minutes I decided to drop it and just walked on, following my instincts.

Right away, I found a shortcut to my "own" street, one that I had used when I was afraid of the Nazis and was trying to escape from the horror.[7] Using this shortcut, I didn't need to go out onto the main streets, but could just walk through a back yard behind the Stephan's Dome.[8] That turned out to be the way from my parents' apartment, too.

One night, while still in Vienna, I went straight into an altered state of consciousness, reliving the memories about the night when I was arrested and forced to go to Buchenwald. First, I "saw" swastikas and flags all over town, and it was just awful. Then I knew I couldn't hide anymore, and I could hear the boots of the soldiers walking in the streets . . . It was as if I were wandering around Vienna in two time periods at once. My body was still in 1993, but my spirit was back in the Nazi time. In this strange state of flashback reality, I drove "madly" around Vienna for some time.

And it all came back to me. How the soldiers arrived early in the morning, four or five of them, including one who was supposedly my friend. How my children were so quiet and big-eyed with terror. How I took a red ribbon from Naima in the lorry. How we were standing together at the railway station, until one German soldier came and took the children away, while another grabbed me from behind and shoved me up onto the train . . .

Scene after scene flashed before my eyes. I cried, but I forced myself to live through these memories, because I knew it was the only way to become free.

After a while, it was all over. Once again I could see Vienna as it is today. And suddenly, I also understood why I had been so afraid of vomiting in the streets. I saw the connection between my past life and this life, and how, all the time, I was frightened to be discovered as a Jew. In that life, I did not "look like a Jew," and I was married to an SS officer. That helped me survive, at least as long as he was alive. But I paid a high price for that safety.

Now, I could see the roots of my current social problems, my phobias and fears about being on the streets with other people. And I knew how to work on this problem in my daily life.

Today I still feel the fear sometimes, when I am very tired or upset or sad. But mostly I live a very normal life now. Sometimes it is a little bit hard for me to stand up and speak in front of a lot of people, but I know I have to make it. Once I get up there and start, it's OK for me. Whenever I feel the fear coming on, I tell myself that I am not Anna-Maria Kellerman from Vienna anymore, I am Lena-Marie Broman now. Then I avoid the panic.

In a way, it's wonderful to see how all of my terrible memories from that life can help me today and to understand why things are as they are. Carl (the therapist) and I are working together in Uppsala, Sweden, where I am a holistic therapist, using aromatherapy, past-life memories, and healing. I have also developed the ability to see auras, that is, psychic colors around people. This is something rather new for me, but very helpful in my work.

I feel that I am well on my way to healing deep inside myself, and I have to admit that, without all of those memories, I would have been only half a person. I had to connect Anna-Maria with Lena-Marie, because we *really are* one and the same. I could not live without all those frightening memories, because, in a way, I am those memories—they are a part of my lives.

And so, the phoenix bird rises from the ashes and flies into the unknown, without pain and fear, but with love!

Chapter 4:

Hands from the Holocaust

by David R. Moffatt

A few days earlier, I had stood with several recent acquaintances in the Jewish cemetery of Lodz, Poland.[1] The place contains many monuments, most of them commemorating World War II atrocities. At one, a sign reads: "Remain quiet and remember the dead." I photographed the monument while one of my friends, a Polish Catholic woman named Joanna, translated.

Those words had reminded me that I was not in a tourist site, although I was acting like a tourist. "I feel strange taking pictures here," I said.

"But it's your job!" Joanna said with a smile. "You are forgiven, of course."

As we walked through another part of the cemetery a short time later, she said, "You know, there is no family in Poland who did not lose someone in the camps. My mother was in Auschwitz, and my grandparents died there." I did not know what to say.

Now, on March 25, 1992, I stood facing another sign, this one reading in five languages: "You are entering a place of exceptional horror and tragedy. Please show your respect for the memory of those who suffered and died here by behaving in a manner appropriate to their memory." A graveled path led past the sign toward a steel gate set into a high barbed-wire fence—the main gate of Auschwitz.

I had come with Wanda, another Polish friend, not as a tourist seeking morbid thrills, but as a haunted man hoping to identify and perhaps placate a series of personal ghosts. By seeking them in the waking world, I hoped to lay them to rest.

A portion of my family is German. Several family members fled Nazi Germany before the war. Legend has it that they baked the family jewels into a fruitcake to save them from confiscation. But others remained behind, and among them was Erich Raeder, Grand Admiral of the Nazi navy until 1943. He was among the defendants at Nuremburg and served ten years in Spandau Prison. I do not believe in collective guilt. But whenever I see films or photos from the Holocaust, I am reminded that those unfathomable horrors were defended by my ancestors.

My visit to Poland had been planned for nearly eight months, and Auschwitz had been on the itinerary the entire time. Several months before departure, my anxiety over the planned visit carried over into my sleeping life, and I awakened from a strange and terrifying dream:

> It was night. I was being driven in a long, black car through darkened streets toward a silhouetted skyline of towers and walls from which searchlights stabbed in every direction. The driver took us through a barbed-wire gate past fences and rows of wooden barracks. He stopped before a building which resembled a barn.

> I was forced to get out of the car by a woman in uniform accompanied by two soldiers. They escorted me into the barn-like building. Several long rows of cubicles or cages made of sheets of steel filled the room. Each was perhaps six feet square, with a small opening on one side. From each opening protruded the head of a child. The place was filthy; excrement covered the floor and walls. The children's faces were smeared with it.
>
> I was given a rag by the uniformed woman and ordered to clean the faces of the children.
>
> But the rag was too small and the task too great. I succeeded only in making them miserable and myself utterly filthy.

At that point I awakened, sweating. As the following weeks passed, I wondered if I would find the site of the nightmare in Poland.

It was not in Auschwitz. There was much to see there, but all was covered with plastic for preservation or recreated in areas where the Germans had managed to destroy evidence of their crimes. A hot dog stand and a souvenir shop stood beside the parking lot. There was something artificial about it all. The phrase "Reader's Digest Condensed Holocaust" ran through my mind again and again.

The camp museum's displays of shoes, suitcases, human hair, and other artifacts were indeed horrible, but I had read about them many times before. Seeing them in person made little impression. Numerous birds perching in the trees along the eaves of the buildings attracted more attention. I had read once that birds do not sing in Auschwitz, but all of these were in full song.

My cynicism peaked when Wanda and I strayed from the main tourist path. Behind the "Wall of Death," where

40,000 people were executed and to which thousands now come to remember the dead, we came upon a trash heap. The low mound was filled with candleholders, drying flowers, and small Israeli flags—loving tributes left the day before and now casually cleared away to make room for the next day's accumulation. I photographed the pitiful remains from several angles.

We walked back through the camp. A building near the gate is now used as a movie theater, and the English language version of a documentary about Auschwitz would be showing soon. The day was dark and windy. Intermittent rain splashed in our faces. As we walked the streets between the dingy barracks, a window slammed open with sufficient force that one of its panes shattered.

We were alone on the street. The sudden sound was a powerful shock. I jumped, startled, and Wanda cried out. But it was only the wind, we assumed, and so we moved on to the theater.

A short time later, as I was watching the movie (which proved to be a mostly familiar collection of grainy black-and-white film footage), the hair began to rise on the back of my neck. *The wind had been in our faces as we walked toward the theater.* The window that had slammed open had swung away from us, *against the wind.*

I was determined to go back for another look. After the movie, I told Wanda I wanted to take another photo and walked back into the camp alone. I had no trouble finding the window that had flown open—it was at the rear of a building which stood directly beside an odd structure constructed of wooden posts and lengths of railroad rail. Later, I learned that the structure was the collective gallows, from which as many as a dozen inmates were hanged simultaneously. When we had walked past it earlier, I had half-heartedly thought of attempting a few chin-ups on the bar; its height was nearly perfect. Now I thought no more of such things.

The shattered window was closed and locked. Hoping to take a look inside the building, I circled around to its front. It was locked and, as far as I could tell, empty, not open to the public.

I was no longer a tourist. I had been touched by the horror that the very name "Auschwitz" represents, and the warning of the shattered window wiped the sneer from my mind. What had swung it open—so impossibly against the wind!—just as I happened to walk past? I bowed my head, resolving to behave more respectfully from then on.

I hurried back to rejoin Wanda, and we spent a few more minutes visiting some final points of interest in the camp. Among them was the gas chamber, a place I remember only as being very damp and very cold. Someone had left a lit candle beside the door. When I bent close to it, I felt no warmth.

Auschwitz had not been the place I had seen in my dream. But two miles away lay the crumbling compound of Auschwitz II-Birkenau, the largest of Hitler's extermination camps. We walked along a main road, turned onto another, crossed a bridge over several rail lines, and there it was, rising out of the gray afternoon. The ominous gate and guardhouse rendered familiar by countless photographs but still alien and sinister to the eye. I wondered what we would find beyond it.

Just inside the gate, we found a sign identical to that in Auschwitz, cautioning us to behave ourselves. There was no need for that warning now. We walked slowly and wordlessly into the nearly two-mile-wide compound, and once again, I wanted to bow my head. Only a few other tourists were visible. The place was silent. Here and there, birds perched on barbed-wire fences or on the wires of a modern power line which crosses the camp.

But I do not remember ever hearing bird song there.

In Birkenau, there was little attempt to create a showcase for tourists. The camp remains largely as it was when the Soviet Army liberated the last remaining prisoners in 1945. Less than one quarter of the original buildings still stand. Rows of crumbling chimneys receding into the distance mark the locations of others destroyed by the liberated or their liberators.

In Auschwitz, flower beds had been planted beside many of the former barracks. There had been no attempt to beautify Birkenau for tourists. A few small signs directed visitors to various points of interest. Several barracks revealed traces of recent activity, some of it by filmmakers who had used Birkenau in several movies. On the wall of one building, a sign marked drawings made by a prisoner. In most of the others, one found graffiti in many languages and of widely varying propriety. A frightening amount of it is anti-Semitic.[2]

The camp is divided into several compounds, each separated from the others by tall barbed-wire fences. As Wanda and I passed through the gate between two areas, I reached out to grasp the wire. It was cold and lifeless to my touch. Fifty years ago, it had carried 400 volts; the slightest touch meant death.

Most of the buildings stood open and empty. We walked through one after another, past sagging rows of wooden three-high bunks, past crumbling brick fireplaces, communal toilets, and long trough-like sinks. Everything was cold, damp, and indescribably silent. I read later that the wooden buildings had originally been prefabricated horse barns, and there was something frighteningly farm-like about it all. But I did not find the building I had visited in my dream, nor did I discover a skyline resembling that which I had "seen" illuminated by searchlights.

As we left one of the buildings, one of my feet settled deeper into the earth than it should have. A hole was revealed when I pulled away, an old sewer or drain collapsing into the swampy soil. On the pathway leading into another of the buildings, a scrap of black cloth lay trampled into the road. It proved to be a *yarmulke* (Jewish skullcap).

The sole major concession to formally memorializing the dead of Birkenau stands at the rear of the camp, between the ruins of two gas chambers, at the end of the rail line which now terminates at an eternal flame. It is an ugly monument of stone blocks and symbolic tombstones, surrounded by a low platform of cobblestones. I was tired of the dreary buildings, frightened that another pitfall might lie beneath my next step. We turned toward the monument.

We walked beside the rusting rail line, along the ramp where half-dead prisoners had stumbled from trains day and night after journeys of a week or more across Eastern Europe. We passed wooden guard towers and the place where Dr. Mengele had stood to dispense life or death with a wave of the hand to the right or left. More fences. Barbed wire was everywhere, much of it fallen from the insulators to lie coiled and rusting on the ground. I had joked before departing for Poland that I planned to bring back a piece of Auschwitz barbed wire as a souvenir. But while I was there, the thought never crossed my mind.

We were walking into the wind again as we approached the monument. The sky remained low; from time to time, drops of rain splattered on our faces and clothing. As we neared the gray stone conglomeration, *I began to feel pressed back by something that was stronger than the wind.* The sensation grew as we walked on, until I felt as if I were walking against a vast sheet of balloon rubber, which was drawing taut and about to fling me back. In my ears was a strange sensation, like that of countless voices crying out a message that could only be one of great fear. I did not actually hear them; I sensed them, as one continues to sense an explosion in one's ears for some moments after the original sound has died away. But they were voices; I am sure of that.

I was unnerved and turned to Wanda, hoping to defuse the situation with words. But before I could speak, she turned to me and said, "I don't like this. It feels like someone is pushing me."

The hair rose on my neck again. We stood on the spot where a million or more had died in the gas chambers fifty years before. We listened to them scream and felt their struggles to push us back.

We did not linger at the monument. No one had been there in days. A rose had been laid on each of the symbolic tombstones, but each was faded and withered. I remember the sound of the wind and the sensation of those voices that were not quite voices. From far outside the camp I heard crowing roosters, traffic, and more than once, a barking dog. But when I remarked to Wanda at how quiet it was, I had to shout to be understood.

We walked back though the huge compound and several more buildings. I had originally planned to spend the entire day exploring Birkenau; now, I did not wish to linger. Whenever I turned my back to the monument and gas chamber ruins, I felt invisible hands hurrying me on my way.

Inside one of the brick buildings, I paused for a moment, sitting down on the edge of one of the tiered bunks. I had walked at least six miles and was facing more; my head spun with fatigue and with confusion born of the day's experiences. I reached up to brush a stray lock of hair from my face and, as I did, I noticed a trickle of blood running down my palm.

When I had grasped the barbed wire, shortly after we entered the camp, I had run one of its prongs deep into the flesh. I looked at the tiny wound and marveled that I had felt no pain.

I wanted no more of the place. We hurried to the gate, past the watchtowers, the barracks, the rail siding where a crew was spreading gravel in preparation for the filming of *Schindler's List.* The invisible hands remained with us, hurrying our steps though the voices which accompanied them faded as we approached the gate. When we stepped through it, the strange sense of being pushed abruptly stopped.

Several days after that eerie afternoon, I met with Joanna again, who asked about my visit. Though I omitted many details, I mentioned some of the strange experiences that Wanda and I had shared. Joanna nodded knowingly.

"Oh yes," she said, "I went there once with my mother, and it was very strange. Sometimes we felt as if someone was still there."

I agreed. I was about to tell Joanna what I had told no one—my reason for visiting the camp, my unease at my German ancestry. But then she spoke again.

"You know, David, there were not only bad Germans there. When my mother was there, she was made to work on a road. One day she was sick and she would have died, but one of the guards threw down his rifle and took her shovel. He did her work that day. They would have killed him if they knew, but he saved my mother's life."

The time did not seem right to discuss my family history. My unease had faded in the wake of my visit to Auschwitz, and in that moment it vanished completely, never to return. The ghosts in Auschwitz are not angry ghosts. They sought not to accuse, but to warn me away from a place they could not know was no longer dangerous. They are deeply frightened, and my only regret is that I could offer no comfort to them.

Several weeks after my return to the United States, I received a small confirmation that something out of the ordinary really had occurred during my visit to the concentration camp. I had taken a number of photos on the grounds of both Auschwitz and Birkenau, all of them using a familiar camera which has been my constant companion since 1982. Its exposure meter had been left on automatic throughout the day, and the lighting conditions—cloudy and dim—were not of the sort to cause any problem with automatic exposure.[3]

Nevertheless, many of the photos I took in Auschwitz and Birkenau were woefully underexposed. All of the photos of Auschwitz were fine, save for those of the trash heap I had photographed with such a jaded eye. In Birkenau, all of the photos taken after I began to feel the strange sensation of being pushed were underexposed. Yet a photo taken seconds after I left the camp was perfect, as were hundreds of others which followed during the trip. But during the period of time when those invisible hands and not-quite-silent voices had tried to warn me away, only one frame (of the monument) was even close to proper exposure.[4] The thought occurred to me that I had been permitted a single souvenir of the place.

Neither Auschwitz nor Birkenau revealed the site of the horrible "barn" I visited in my dream. To this day, I wonder if the place ever actually existed.[5] But I will not search for it anymore. The wound in my hand healed cleanly, but left a little white scar. I believe in ghosts now, and I remember. It is, I now realize, the best I can do. "Those who will not remember the past," wrote George Santayana in a passage often quoted about Auschwitz, "are condemned to repeat it."

Chapter 5:

The White Rose

by Judith Hart

In 1990, a spiritual awakening catapulted me forward and backward in time, to places yet to be explored and centuries long past. A spontaneous "kundalini" awakening had precipitated my abilities of clairvoyance, clairaudience, mediumship, and spiritual healing. At that time I took a new name—Judith—to honor the Jewish part of myself, for I have been an Essene healer in several other lifetimes. In addition, "Judith" also honors my many times great-grandmother, a Cherokee Indian who was given the name Judith when she was raised by the Quakers.

Life was mystical, frightening, and confusing for me during that initial period of learning how to use these old-new abilities. While researching my family genealogy, I always had the feeling that a trail of ancestral spirits was following me. Eventually I came to love and honor them as my teachers. Also during that time, many past-life memories surfaced with a strong sense of familiarity.

My first "flashback" Holocaust memory came in March of 1993, two months before I was to visit the new United States Holocaust Memorial Museum. I say "flashback," because the scene I saw was very vivid, and the power of the emotional response was enough to send me into a torrent of tears. My anguish was not so much for me as for my mother in that life, who was pregnant with me as a fetus and who was also suffering terrible mental trauma over her separation from her husband and two male children after deportation to a death camp. Her suffering was so great that I could feel the emotional impact of her misery from within the womb.

This flashback was powerful. For days afterward, I was in a state of emotional delicacy where I felt prone to sudden tears and depression. The impact was such that I had a driving desire to visit the Holocaust Memorial Museum in Washington, D.C., to grieve the memories of my ancestors from another life.

Because of the huge crowds desiring to visit the new museum, I could not get tickets for over a month. During the interim weeks of waiting, I had a most unforgettable spiritual experience in preparation for my trip.

I was alone one evening, when I suddenly felt a sense of urgency, as if something or someone were trying to make contact with me. Having had these experiences before, I knew that going into a meditative state would be the most conducive way to become receptive. As I did so, I immediately felt myself being drawn into a different time and dimension. Then I "saw" myself standing in a beer cellar in Germany. Through the darkness and gloom, I could barely make out the outlines of a group of people hiding behind the beer vats.

As I moved closer to them, a great wave of fear and despair washed over me, and I began to cry as though my heart would break. I realized that I was witnessing a family of Jews who were being hidden in this German cellar to avoid their arrest and deportation to prison camps and certain death.

The family came out from behind the vats and spoke to me. They indicated who they were and their circumstances. They were the remaining members of a family of six, now only four in number. There was a grandmother, a young wife and her husband, and a little boy about ten years old. The grandfather and the youngest child had died in the first weeks of hiding.

The family went on to relate their experiences of being hidden by a German family and how the house had been restructured to hide the entrance to the beer cellar. They remained hidden during the course of the war. Their second child also died. When the war was over, the couple emigrated to America, and the grandmother stayed behind, living with the German family who had hidden them for all those years. Now, decades later, all of them were dead, but still earthbound.

Their purpose in contacting me now, the family explained, was for me to help them leave their trauma behind. They no longer wanted to be held to the earth plane through scarring memories and bitterness. They asked if I would accompany them, in the spirit, to meet their ancestors who were waiting for them. I agreed to do this.

We moved together as a group of spirits toward the light, which was becoming more and more evident. Then I saw hundreds of spirit beings and received the impression that these were their ancestors from generations before, who had come to meet the family and welcome them beyond the "mortal veil." There was great joy and exaltation!

Before the family turned to leave, they thanked me profusely for my help, then asked me to take a white rose to the Holocaust Museum in their memory. This I agreed to do.

On the day that I finally went to Washington, D.C., I bought a lovely white rose. I carried my rose on the underground Metro trains, then into the museum building, and through the many floors and corridors. Feeling the most profound respect for those who had fought in the Warsaw ghetto resistance, I laid my white rose beneath the exhibit about their brave uprising. Then I proceeded on.

Shortly thereafter, I was stunned to see another exhibit called "The White Rose." This was the name of a resistance group of young German men and women, who had opposed Nazism and the cruelty to the Jews. The members of the White Rose movement were subsequently arrested, interrogated by the Gestapo, and executed. I was profoundly moved by that exhibit, and the "coincidence" of the white flower that I had so lovingly carried.[1]

* * *

After that amazing series of experiences in April and May of 1993, I had a steady stream of "Holocaust victim" spirits visiting me for about a year. For a while, it was like an "underground railroad" in my home, with entire Jewish families coming through and asking for help in leaving this plane of consciousness. It was with profound respect and joy that I embarked with them upon many ventures in spiritual healing. I had received the grace to heal not only my own past lives, but also the consciousness of others with a similar need.

Why was I "chosen" for this work? Perhaps because, although I am not Jewish in this lifetime, many of my past lives were as devout Jews in times of persecution. In addition to the life as an Essene healer mentioned above, I have memories of fleeing Jerusalem at the time of the burning and desecration of the Temple, and of the Zealots resisting the Romans at Masada. I also remember being an Eastern European Jew at a time when there were pogroms, although I do not remember directly experiencing them. Nevertheless, because of these memories, Judaism is deeply ingrained in my soul.

However, I had experienced persecution in so many of those incarnations that I had developed a type of "victim consciousness" within myself, a lingering sense of being persecuted in various capacities. Naturally, this is an easy pattern of thinking to fall into, when one is constantly being singled out as a target for hatred. Not only did I have this experience as a Jew in past lives, but also as a Catholic monk, as a witch burned at the stake in Europe, and as a black slave in the American South.

A major part of my soul healing has come through exploring the attitude that Jews have about life and the great value that Judaism places on each individual life. Understanding the intense will to live that many Jews have had in the face of destitution has brought about a major change in me and has helped me to establish a strong will to live and embrace life. I was helped in this work by one of my spirit guides, Rabbi Joseph Hellerman, who always brings a wonderful sense of pleasure and joy of living.

Today, I have fewer Jewish spirits coming to me for healing. It could be that once the Holocaust Museum was completed, its very existence released the Jewish spirits to move on, knowing that the museum now bears witness so that the world can never forget. It might also be that my own memories of Jewish lifetimes are fading with my healing of Holocaust issues and work with global consciousness.

As both a psychotherapist and a healer who works with spirit beings in other dimensions, I understand that this process has now moved away from viewing time as "linear" toward the idea that, on certain levels of vibrational frequencies, there really is no time or space. In the higher spiritual planes, all things move together in a grand flow. Perhaps we are really living several incarnations simultaneously and effecting changes in all of them through the healing that takes place in this one. Be that as it may, my own life is enriched by the joy that I receive in helping to climinate the pain and suffering that has too long been such a part of humanity's experience on earth. *L'chaim, l'chaim*—to life!

Chapter 6:

More Than a Fairy Tale

by Marcia Hollabaugh

My early childhood years were idyllic, and I remember them with great fondness. Mine was a very normal life during the 1950s in America, with wonderful back yards, musical instruments, art projects, parties, and children's TV programs. Up until the age of six, the biggest disappointment in my entire life had been the death of my little white pet mouse. Other than that, I can see nothing in this tranquil existence that would explain the terrifying Holocaust images which haunted me from a very early age.

During my growing-up years, my family lived in three different houses in Pennsylvania: one near Philadelphia, and the other two near Pittsburgh. It was at the house near Philadelphia, when I was only four years old, that I began to notice how I could envision "another world" in my mind's eye—a world that appeared sinister and hideous, in contrast to my peaceful surroundings in Pennsylvania. Over a period of several years, this other world, which was shrouded in darkness and mystery, gradually revealed itself to me through a series of visions, dreams, and daydreams.

One day, at the age of four, I was playing alone in the living room. Suddenly I found myself—in my mind's eye—standing in front of a huge multi-storied brick building. The building had two odd vertical columns of windows and appeared to be in an unattractive and bizarre-looking "city," with no people, animals, cars, or plants. On another occasion, I "saw" a huge, looming, dark-colored complex of buildings against a dark brown sky.

Years later, I would come to recognize these images when I viewed photographs of the Nazi concentration camps.[1] But as a four-year-old child, growing up in tranquil Pennsylvania, I had no explanation for this other world. My family was Protestant at the time (we later became Unitarians), and I am of Anglo-German descent. There was never any talk of Jews or concentration camps in my home.

* * *

In my kindergarten year, we moved to Pittsburgh. About this same time, another detail was added to the sombre vision of the strange "city." I remember coming home from school one day and, while standing in the kitchen, I "saw" the industrial complex under a dark brown sky again—*only this time, I could hear the sound of a siren!* I looked out the window and wondered how I could be hearing a siren that seemed to have no discernible source.

Because Pittsburgh is a "steel city," the reader may wonder if the sight of the factories in real life had triggered my childhood visions. That's a good question. However, we did not live in Pittsburgh proper, but in a suburban area outside the city. Not until much later did I actually see Pittsburgh's steel mills.

These images appeared somewhat randomly during my childhood, and I did not automatically connect them together at the time. One day, when I was about five or six, I suddenly "saw" myself in what I thought was a fairy tale:

> There was a big, black, hideous Castle, with a strange roof. The clouds were gray and ominous, hanging low in the sky. A smaller rectangular building was parallel to the Black Castle, and a smaller row of buildings was lined up at a right angle to it. One of these little buildings had an open door. I peeked through the door into a tiny room that looked like a closet and saw a pale-looking Woman standing there, with no clothes on, and her back to me.

What a strange story this is, I thought to myself. Where are the king and queen in this fairy tale?

Then in the summer of 1960, just before entering the first grade, I had a waking vision that shattered my peaceful childhood forever. All of a sudden, while I was lying in bed waiting to fall asleep, I saw myself in that other world:

> I was kneeling in a tiny little "shed" that was built out of vertically arranged, four-inch wooden slats, about eight feet high. The shed was only three feet wide and three feet deep, and my wrists were tied to a pole that ran vertically through the center of the shed and passed between my forearms and thighs. When I looked down at myself in the vision, I was no longer a child. I was an unclothed woman!

> It felt like a warm summer night. Through the cracks in the slats I saw, to my left, a building with an odd-shaped roof that had little square lit-up windows. To my right was a smaller rectangular building, while the area in front of me, between the two buildings, was lit up by the orange glow of electric lights on poles in the background.
>
> Somewhere in front of me, at a fair distance off to the left, I heard much noise, as if people were walking around and sound waves were bouncing off large walls in front of me. I also heard somebody approaching from my right and coming towards me. Suddenly a door opened up behind me—I could hear the hinges on the right—and an orange light was shone into the tiny shed. Then somebody started beating my back with a whip!

As suddenly as it had begun, this horrible vision ended. I was back in my six-year-old body, and I was petrified. An hour passed before the adrenaline rush began to subside, and I was finally able to calm down.

Between the ages of six and eight, I consistently had some variation of this vision almost every night. Little by little, more details revealed themselves. Just before falling asleep, I would envision myself in a dreamlike state, where I would be walking on a path near my house in Pittsburgh, through a woods that consisted of *a mixture of deciduous and pine trees.*[2] I would walk until I was standing in a clearing that was in the other world. In front of me would be not just one shed, but a row of five sheds. I would stand in front of the fifth shed on the far right, just as someone was coming towards the shed from my right, carrying a whip. Then this person would open the door and start beating the woman sitting in the shed.

On other occasions, the scene of the beating changed, and I would walk in the woods until I saw the sheds in the opening in the woods. Eventually, the person with the whip stopped coming, and I would just see the sheds aligned in the forest beside the trail.

Next to our first Pittsburgh house, there was a little wooded area where I often played. Lying across the path was a dead tree with no bark, which had fallen long ago. Sitting alone on this old log, I would contemplate the strange images of the other world. Somehow, my mind formed a strong association between the terrifying beating in the vision and the dead tree in real life. Even in my adult years, long after the dark visions of childhood had faded from memory, I still saw that image of the dead tree lying in the woods. Well into my thirties, I had nightmares about somebody beating me beside a tree stump.

* * *

In addition to the Woman in the Shed, there was another image which haunted me during my childhood. In the spring of 1961, at the age of six, just after we moved to our second house in Pittsburgh, I saw a barbershop pole for the first time. I was very, very apprehensive about it.

"What is this *thing?*" I asked my mother.

"That's a barbershop pole," she replied.

"What is a barbershop?"

"That's a place where men get their hair cut."

I did not totally believe my mother. In my child's mind, I equated the red-and-white striped pole with something frightening. For some unknown reason, the image of the pole gave me a feeling of extreme anxiety.

Eight months later, during the autumn of my second-grade year, the motif of the "barbershop pole" appeared to me in what would be, even to this day, the strangest dream of my life. One night, when I was totally asleep in bed, I dreamed that I actually became the woman in the visions:

> Dressed in baggy gray pants and a shirt, I was with a group of people walking on a sidewalk. Parallel to the sidewalk (to our immediate right) was a huge, white, old three-story building with many windows. Suddenly I noticed, right in front of me, a *thing* which was about my own height—a tiny little house, set at an angle, with spiraling stripes on it. This strange thing was brightly colored, with blue and green alternating stripes (resembling a barbershop pole) that contrasted with the gray, low-hanging clouds which permeated the atmosphere of the dream . . .
>
> Turning right, we walked into the building, went up an ornate staircase to the top floor, turned right again, and walked down a wide hallway. The floor appeared to be black marble. On our right, we passed two closed doors, which opened inwardly. We also went through a door that opened inwardly (with hinges on the right side) into a small modern office . . .

To this day, the details of that office remain clear in my mind: the map on the wall, two flags in the corner, a bookcase, the large desk with chairs that had curved seats . . . An official-looking person came into the room, and several of us talked with him. He sat at the desk, while we sat in front of him, in the chairs. Then the scene shifted, and the dream continued with the same incredible detail:

> Once again, I was with a group of people in baggy clothes, walking on a path through a wooded area. The sun was on my right, shining through the leaves, as we came to a big, square, two-story building, well-built of tan-colored stone, with a "ridge" of some sort up at the upper perimeter of the top floor.

From my childish perspective, I thought that this building was an old German castle with a rampart—the "ridge" on top. Again, it seemed like something out of a strange fairy tale. That may account for the next part of the dream, in which I entered a "throne room" where we were made to stand in rows, in front of ten little tables, which were in front of the "German King" sitting on his throne. We were ordered to "bow before the German King." As we started to bow, another group of people came up behind us and began beating us all with whips. I clearly remember that the person who was beating me was standing to my left. Then the dream continued:

> I seemed to be in a maze, which was inside of a building that had no windows and consisted of long hallways with walls that were grayish white. I turned around and tried to get out of the maze, but realized that I was trapped . . .
>
> Then I was with a small group of people in a field that was bordered by a forest, *which was a mixture of deciduous and pine trees.* The sun was behind us and it was still summer, as the grass and trees were green . . . There was a small white house in front of us . . .
>
> Next we were in front of a door. A man in front of me opened the door. As we entered what I thought was a large cave, I looked over to my right. In the

background I could see a corner of the little white cottage in the field.

When we entered the large cave, I noticed that there were other little "caves" inside the big "cave." Each of the little "caves" had an entrance that was shaped like an inverted "U" or the opening to a tunnel. People were lying in the little "caves," with their heads facing outward toward the center of the room. I could see the tops of their heads. The dream ended with me lying face up in a tiny little "tunnel" that was made out of a porous tan substance.

Years later, I would recognize this scene with the "caves" and the little white cottage when I saw photographs of Crematorium IV and the white house gas chamber at Auschwitz.[3] Each of the ovens had a rounded door that resembled the entrance to a tunnel, and the "caves" themselves were lined with fire brick. But as a child, I did not see the people as corpses. I only knew that the scene was something incredibly bizarre. Why, I wondered, were these adults taking naps during the daytime?

* * *

In 1970, while I was still in high school, I attended some meetings with the Edgar Cayce study group in Pittsburgh. I began to read a great deal of literature about Edgar Cayce, reincarnation, and books on Eastern religion. Through this association, I considered the possibility that I may have had a previous life in Nazi Germany. But, quite frankly, I was not interested in pursuing the issue in depth. I spoke of it to no one and gradually forgot about the whole thing.

My life moved on. I graduated from high school, went to college, and became a musician. I also continued my interest in spiritual things, including astrology and Native American prophecies. Yet the thread of the Holocaust kept reappearing, weaving its way in and out of my life many times, as if to remind me that the story wasn't over yet.

In January of 1989, I returned to academia after a long absence. In February of that same year, after a long period of insomnia, I saw "her" again in a lucid color vision—the Woman! Only this time, as an adult, I knew it was no fairy tale! Needless to say, I was traumatized over this vision for months afterward. I even went to see a psychologist, which turned out to be fruitless.

Then, in a music history class, I encountered an opera written in response to the Holocaust by Arnold Schoenberg, a modern Jewish composer and a Zionist. While studying the score and a recording of his opera *Moses and Aaron,* I had a strange dream:

> I was in an American Jewish temple, facing the Star of David, which was rendered in blue and white tile work over the altar. Instead of a cantor, the temple had a choir of women singers who stood to the right of the altar and sang in Hebrew. After the singing was over, I went with the people into another room. They were very happy to see me.

At the time I wondered, why would I dream of being in a Jewish temple? I never had any desire to study Judaism, and a "Jewish temple" was only something I had seen in photographs.[4] I also wondered about the significance of the women singers in the dream.

Then in the winter of 1994, I saw Steven Spielberg's film, *Schindler's List.* I was filled with great trepidation, especially during the scene where a crowd of women prisoners is standing together naked, waiting to enter the "showers" at Auschwitz. I responded very, very deeply to that scene. In response to my deep feelings about it, I went to a discussion of the film at the local Jewish temple.

During the discussion, a woman who had converted to Judaism told how she had "cellular memories" of being a Jew and had never been comfortable in her parents' church. She planned to go to Russia and find out about her Jewish ancestors, particularly a Yiddish-speaking grandmother. As she told her story, I pondered whether I, too, might have "cellular memories" of being a Jew in the Holocaust.[5]

After that, some of the details of my childhood dreams returned, and I began to search for historical evidence. When I examined the photo album called *Auschwitz: A History in Photographs*,[6] I saw a whipping bench that looked like the "little tables" in my dream about the German King. I also read an account of how prisoners were punished by being forced to spend the night in "standing cells" on Cell Block 11 at Auschwitz. That was the first time I had ever heard of a "standing cell." But when I tried to find proof of the five wooden sheds in my visions, they were nowhere to be found.

I actually breathed a sigh of relief. Perhaps this was not the place I saw in my childhood dreams after all. I really hoped it was somewhere else—anyplace but Auschwitz! Yet the more I studied, the more I was able to confirm my Holocaust "memories."

Finally, on February 24, 1995, in a grainy photograph of the large white administration building at Auschwitz, I found the striped "thing" which had triggered my fear of the barber pole. It was a little guard house.[7] After I made this connection, all the other pieces quickly fell into place. I now believe that I was Marta Kushner, a German Jewish woman in her early twenties, who died at

Auschwitz-Birkenau sometime around July 1944 and was reborn into my present body in 1954.

At times, I still ask myself, are these memories really reincarnation, or is there another theory which will explain them? Will I ever heal from the deep wounds that these past-life experiences have carved into my soul?

Looking back over my life, I can now see that there have already been some stages of healing. The first step began with the wonderful, dark forests of Pennsylvania. After I had begun to see the woman in the shed from my past life, the Pennsylvania trees, very quietly and persistently, began to take over my dreams, replacing the terrifying forest of Auschwitz.

In my childhood, I associated the frightening "other world" with that dead tree in Pittsburgh. Metaphorically, the dead tree has come back to life. Now, I meditate upon visualizations of trees, which help me to deal with the painful past-life memories. Sometimes I imagine the cosmic Tree of Life as a huge, white tree, blossoming with many red flowers. At other times, I visualize a peaceful Sequoia forest with moss. There is something very healing about these beautiful images of trees.

Another type of healing has come from my association with classical music. My career as a musician got started at the age of six or seven, when my parents bought me an old upright piano. I would gaze into the intricate patterns in the grain of the wood while I was playing and would enter a beautiful realm of consciousness—almost a meditative state. This was a welcome relief from the shattering memories of the woman in the shed. Through the structure of music, I metaphorically re-created a mandala of myself.

As I look to the future, I would now like to create some form of artistic ceremonialism, a musical piece which will address my own experience. Although it has truly been a grueling effort to write this article, it has also been an enormous release of emotional energy. Now I plan to carry that energy forward and transform it into creativity. I want to write a beautiful piece of music—with chamber orchestra and a women's choir—in memory of the tens of thousands of women who died at Auschwitz-Birkenau.

Chapter 7:

Each One Has a Name

by Diana Lubarsky

I grew up as a Conservative Jew in New York, knowing only the basics about my religious heritage. As for reincarnation, I didn't actually believe in it—but then again, I never really disbelieved, either. I found the subject interesting. As long as I wasn't asked to sign a contract about my beliefs, I just mused and listened, with an inner feeling that immediately classified the stories I heard as either "possible" or "hogwash." There was no precise guideline, just a sense of plausibility versus neurosis.

My personal experience with reincarnation began after the birth of my first child, Joshua, in 1974. I was twenty-nine years old at the time. On many nights I would wake up covered in sweat and trembling with a horrible dream still clinging in my mind: the Germans were coming to take my son away, and I was throwing him out the window into the arms of my neighbors in order to save him. This recurring dream had some minor variations, but the story was always essentially the same. When I told it to my husband, Elliot, he was puzzled.

"Why would you dream that?" he asked. "Our neighbors are German, not Jewish."

Next came the sculptures. I am a very tactile person, and I have loved the feel of clay in my fingers as far back as I can remember. I dabbled in clay in Greenwich Village where Elliot and I lived, then at a friend's studio in Mahopac after we moved to Yorktown Heights, fifty miles north of New York City. Over the years, I made a long succession of lopsided pots, bowls, and ashtrays, but nothing you could really call art. Several of my friends sculpted beautifully, almost magically creating ingenious shapes and figures. But I knew I could never do that—or so I thought.

Then one day, shortly after the dreams began, I took a wad of clay and crudely attempted to form the body of a person. With clay, you have to work it several times to get it right, so you can't have instant gratification. After making the initial form, I had to wait until the clay had hardened sufficiently, before I could whittle away the excess material. And lo and behold, a human figure emerged. It was unbelievable, as if a person were inside the lump of clay all along, and I had only to find him!

I immediately began forming Holocaust images. I didn't know why at the time, only that this was what came into my head, heart, and hands. I was possessed by these deep, deep feelings, but I never told anybody that I was creating Holocaust images, because "you don't talk about that." This was back in the 1970s, before the movies and museums, when Jews were only beginning to discuss it in public.[1] I was barely involved with my Judaism in those days and didn't even know much about the Holocaust, other than it had happened, was connected to my people, and was very painful.

Friends at the studio initially asked what I was doing, and I would shrug it off and say, "Oh, I don't know . . . "

But I did know. I knew exactly what I was doing. I just didn't know why.

Sculpture after sculpture emerged, and the Holocaust became understandable to me. I couldn't seem to stop myself, nor could I answer the many questions everyone asked of me: Were you in the Holocaust? (No.) Was your family in the camps? (No.) Did you lose extended family members in Europe? (No.) Just what is your connection to this?

I couldn't answer the questions, but I cried each time a new piece came into my head, because the feelings surrounding each event that I depicted were very painful. I wasn't just making artistic sculptures—I was making real people. I would sit there and mold the figures with my hands, and although they were not always anatomically correct, they had a sense of proportion and movement about them. They "felt" human. They were real individuals, and they were very alive to me.

When I began showing my work, the critics wondered how I could portray the Holocaust so movingly when I had never been there. "She remembers what she never saw," read the 1978 headline in *The Yorktowner,* a local newspaper.[2] Of course, the headline wasn't referring to reincarnation. I had spoken of that to no one. But the "coincidence" was still uncanny. In the article, Sheila Moldaver wrote of my work:

> Memories last a long time. Some memories are not solely our own experience, but are collective. Sometimes it is our own personal experience, sometimes a vicarious one that comes to us by television or radio or film . . . For myself included, images of Hitler and concentration camps and people with faces of death come only from photographs, movies, and books—and yet, the emotional experi-

> ence they convey is as shared, in some ways, as if we had been there . . . Such an experience happened to me when I saw a group of seven sculptures by D.K. Lubarsky entitled "The Holocaust Series."[3]

Among the seven sculptures in that series was "Nameless Faceless Masses," which remains a very important piece today. Back then, if you flipped through books on the Holocaust, you always saw those photos of thousands of people, thousands of skeletons, thousands of bodies piled up. And it was all just a big blur. Nobody ever stopped to think that *each one was a person.* Each one was a soul, each one was born, lived, breathed, and died . . . So I sculpted a mass of people surrounded with barbed wire, and dedicated it to the millions in the blurred photographs who perished in the camps. There are sixty-nine people in this sculpture. Each one is individually posed, and each one has a name.

Where do these images come from? After the first year or two of making these sculptures, I realized that I had access to a psychic doorway into the past. There was a large group of spirit people who seemed to enter my head when I was at rest. I began to communicate with them in my mind, and it was understood between us that I would be a conduit for sculpting what had happened to them. We agreed on this together. When I call upon them for a new sculpture, I receive a steady stream of Holocaust images flooding my mind. Sometimes it's difficult to "freeze frame" the single image that I eventually render in clay.

On several occasions, I have had confirmation that the spirit people who inspired me really did live on earth. Once was when the famous photographer, Roman Vishniac,[4] attended the first exhibit that I ever had. When he saw my work, he was deeply moved. He bought a sculpture—the first major piece I ever sold. Roman then told his wife Edith to go out to the car and bring back a book of his photographs,[5] which he gave me as a gift. Three days later, I opened the book *and saw a photograph of the very same woman whose face was on the sculpture that he purchased.* Was this why Vishniac bought that particular piece? Did he know the woman personally? I do not know.[6]

A similar "coincidence" happened with *Diaspora I.* This piece represents the thread of Jewish continuity, with a Jewish woman bearing a Jewish child, regardless of whether she was raped, her husband was killed, or the village was pillaged. If the mother is Jewish, then the child is Jewish. Years after I created her in sculpture, *I actually found her* in an old Holocaust photo, where a Nazi soldier was pointing a gun at her.[7]

There is a dichotomy of safety and danger that recurs frequently in my work. *In Memory of a Jewish Child, 1938-1948,* looks like a pleasant street scene at first—the sun is shining, everything is golden, there's a little cat eating from her bowl on the front steps . . . That's what the world saw concerning the Jews—a nice facade. But sometimes if you want the truth, you have to turn the corner—and when you do, you see the Jewish child who was thrown away with the trash. The cat on the steps has food to eat, but not the little girl huddled among the garbage cans. Why "1948" instead of "1945," when the war ended? Because in 1948, the state of Israel was founded. At last, there existed a place of refuge for the Jewish children, if only they could get there.

Second Generation was a very difficult piece to do. On one side of the street is the Shema, the central prayer of Judaism: "Hear, O Israel, the Lord is our God, the Lord is One." But on the other side of the street is "Hear, O Israel: Never again! *Zachor*—remember!" It was an extremely painful thing to do, balancing the Shema and the Holocaust. Yet this is the reality of the first generation after the war.

And the second generation? They don't feel the same pain as their parents, so they are happy, carrying their little teddy bears, etc. But look again: They are also lugging this huge swastika, because now, in addition to the Shema, they must carry the memory of the swastika with them. The Shema and the swastika—if the Jews lose either one, they're dead. Future generations will react just as strongly when they see a swastika as when they hear the Shema. The Shema is our religion; the swastika is reality.

Over the years, it became more and more apparent to me that I had been among the victims of the Holocaust in another life, but it was years before I could verbalize that aloud to anyone. *Four Faces* is the only one of my sculptures that is autobiographical, in the sense that this is a self-portrait of my family in the other life. The Hasidic-looking father was my husband, and the mother was I, with their son and daughter. They are surrounded by a heavy chain representing the Holocaust, but the last link is left open, in hope for the sixth commandment: "Thou shalt not kill."

Memories of my past incarnation in the Holocaust revealed themselves to me gradually, over a period of ten years, like a jigsaw puzzle with ten thousand tiny, seemingly disconnected pieces:

> I had lived somewhere in Europe with a husband, and a son, and a daughter. The Nazi reign began. One day, my husband did not come home. Darkness fell. My children and I were rounded up. There was a long train ride, with hay on the floor. An old rabbi and I sat huddled together on the floor of the

train. He blessed me and told me that under no circumstances was I to forget what was happening. *I promised that I would remember.*

The end came in some sort of wooden barracks with dirt floors, very poorly constructed. At the base of one of the posts in the barracks, I found a rock. It was a prized possession, this rock, a very great treasure, because in that place we had absolutely nothing. I knew that my children were dying, and there was no hope for any of us. I had brought them into the world, and now I wanted them to die swiftly by my hand, mercifully, with love and dignity, and without fear.

I told my daughter to kneel, close her eyes, and we would play a game. Then I took the rock and hit her on the back of the head with every ounce of strength that I had left. As I wrapped her tiny, frail body in some cloth that I had, I looked up, and there were other mothers on the bunks watching me, but nobody said a word. Then I called my son and did the same thing. It was the end for me, too—an emotional suicide.

I climbed into the bunk between their bodies and just lay there, waiting for death to come. Time passed. I was taken away with the dead on a cart to the crematoria. There was no pain. The last sight I remember was the flame. I don't remember burning. I don't remember death. It was almost a sense of relief.

Then all of a sudden, it was like I had a rocket under me—I shot all the way up past the clouds into the blue sky, as high and as fast as you can possibly imagine. I was looking downward and it seemed as if the ground and the roof of the building were zooming away from me.

In that life, the Nazis did kill our bodies. But they could not destroy our souls. During the years that I raised my new family in this life, the spirits of the two children from my past life hovered close to me, silent and invisible to all but myself. I nurtured them all with love and protection, until the spirit children were ready to move on into the next world.

I myself remain between two worlds—the Holocaust and the present. Holocaust survivors often sense this. Once, when I was doing an exhibit and they wanted a guest speaker, I located a survivor, and, of course, we began to talk behind the scenes. The more we shared, the more we had in common. In fact, the synchonicity was amazing. Her married name was Siegal and my maiden name was Siegal. Her daughter's name was Riessa and my mother's name was Riessa. She was finishing a book and I was finishing a sculpture. She was writing about the train station at Auschwitz and I was sculpting the train station at Auschwitz . . .

Even though we were physically born in different generations, our lives were running parallel, to the point that *she was liberated in April 1945, and I was born in the same month and year—April 18, 1945!* We couldn't figure the exact time and date, but it was probably within hours—perhaps even minutes—of each other. Although she had come to America in the physical and I had come through reincarnation, we were of the same "generation." That's how it is with me and Holocaust survivors. We look into each other's eyes and we understand each other. Spiritually, we are from the same era.

I have not forgotten my promise to the old rabbi as we sat on the floor of the train in another life, so long ago. I remember what happened. I came to America in the only way that I could, to tell the story with my sculptures and give identities to the nameless, faceless masses:

The one who stands
The one who has fallen
The one who clings to a child
The children who cling to each other
The empty people staring
And the ones who still hope someone
  will come to save them . . .
Each one has a name.

Chapter 8:

Say Kaddish for Us

by Sigrid Dreyfuss-Manelis

I am a child of the Holocaust. Altogether, I lost thirty-six people in my extended family because of Nazi persecution of Jews. On November 10, 1938—*Kristallnacht*—my father was dragged off to the Dachau concentration camp. After about eleven months, by some great miracle, he came out of there alive. Maybe it was because of a child's prayer. You see, I prayed for his return day and night. I had seen him dragged away, and I was later blessed to see him returned to us.

Soon after my father came home, we were able to leave Germany, because my mother could prove her American ancestry to the United States consul in Stuttgart. Her father, the son of an American mother, held dual citizenship—German and American. Because of that, we were given affidavits that helped us get to Holland and then to Philadelphia.

My mother was a descendant of the Winelanders, a prominent Jewish family in Philadelphia. Their lineage goes back many, many years in America—I think they were called "Mayflower Jews."[1] In the mid-nineteenth century, my great-grandmother, Rosa Winelander, went to Germany to visit her relatives. While there, she met and fell in love with great-grandfather Lindauer. She remained there and married him, but she never gave up her American citizenship. Because of that wise decision three generations ago, it was possible for us, her descendants, to escape Nazi Germany.

We left Germany on January 17, 1940, which was practically the last opportunity to cross the Dutch border. From Holland we took the train to Antwerp, Belgium, where we boarded a Dutch ship, the *Westerland,* and headed for Calais, France. From there we crossed the English Channel to Dover and picked up a few American passengers, including an entertainer named "Pegleg" Bates. Then we sailed the Atlantic Ocean to America.

The sea was very rough at that time of year, and we also had to navigate through minefields, so the journey was tense and frightening. "Pegleg" Bates was one of the few passengers who did not succumb to seasickness, so he entertained us to keep our spirits up. Finally, on February 3, 1940, we arrived in New York Harbor. From there we took the train to Philadelphia, where we were met at the station by the American branch of the Winelander-Lindauer family.

The spiritual encounter I will now share is about my mother's sister, Rosa Lindauer Kohn, who was named after my great-grandmother Rosa, the one who had kept her American citizenship. Rosa Kohn was very, very close to me. In many ways, Aunt Rosa was like a second mother. She had lost her own child during pregnancy and was never able to be pregnant again. As a child, I spent many summers with her, and we were together a lot before I left Europe.

Unfortunately, Rosa Kohn did not survive the Nazis.

Even though we had arranged for papers for her and her husband, Lipmann Kohn, to leave Archshofen, Germany, and come to Philadelphia, they never made it. Before we left, Rosa had told my mother, "If I write to you that 'Fräulein Neilah[2] is just around the corner,' that means we are probably going to be taken away."

Seven months after we had arrived in America, near the High Holy Days in the fall of 1940, we did get that devastating message. My mother was very despondent about it, because she loved her sister deeply. My grandmother—Aunt Rosa's mother—dressed completely in black that Yom Kippur. This made a very deep impression on me as a child, because the usual custom for the High Holy Days is to wear new white clothing or some other festive color.

* * *

I often thought about Aunt Rosa over the years, and I would think to myself how much I would like to see her again. I wondered: is there really such a thing as meeting people again after we die? Even as a teenager, I used to think about things like that.

Years later, when I came to Baltimore, I met Olga Worrall and Ambrose Worrall. They were well-known seers, psychics, and writers, etc.[3] We became very close, and I called them "Uncle Ambrose and Aunt Olga." As a matter of fact, even though they were of the Christian faith, they proudly took on the role of grandparents at my son's bar mitzvah. That's how close we were.

One day, as we were just sitting in meditation, something very unusual happened. Aunt Olga all of a sudden said, "Oh my God—Sigrid, there is a lady by the name of Rose—or Rosa—coming through, and she really wants to talk to you."

I got the chills. I felt a strong presence in the room, and I started to feel like I was surrounded by grief. Then I started to cry. Olga Worrall kept saying, "It's Rosa," but that didn't quite fit, because I called my aunt "Tante Rosel," which in German is an endearing term for "Aunt Rosa." But then Olga said to me, "Oh . . . it's like Rosa, but it's not exactly that."

This made sense to me, so I asked, "Does she say she's Tante Rosel?" And Olga said, "Something like that, yes."

With that, I went through some very emotional moments before I could compose myself. Then Olga continued, "She's wailing and she's crying . . . She has no children, she has no place to be buried . . . She and her husband are both here now. And most of all, she's crying because she says she has no *kaddish*."

Kaddish is the Jewish prayer for the dead. It is usually said by the surviving children every day for eleven months after the funeral, then on the anniversary of the death each year. Tante Rosel was apparently trying to tell me that her soul could find no peace, because she never had a proper burial, nor did she and her husband have a living child to say *kaddish* in their memory.

I thought to myself: How in the world could all of this be real? So, for a few moments, I was very hesitant about accepting it. Then all of a sudden Olga said, "She calls you by a different name. She says you will know the name . . . it's something like "Sorelah" or "Sorah . . . " At that moment, I knew this was real, because Tante Rosel used to call me by my Hebrew name: Soreleh bas Esther—Sarah, daughter of Esther. There was no way that Olga could have known that.

This experience was very profound for me, and I decided to do something about it. Although *kaddish* is usually said by one's children, it can also be done by proxy. So I called the Talmudical Academy and arranged for them to have a *kaddish* said regularly for both her and Uncle Lipmann. Although we tried very carefully to research their actual death dates, in the end we could find no records. So we simply chose an annual date on the Jewish calendar, when we would have *kaddish* said for all the members of our family who perished in the Holocaust.

About six months after I arranged for the *kaddish,* I had a powerful dream that was so incredible, so *very real*—I dreamed that Tante Rosel had come to me in spirit. And even though she didn't look happy yet, she said that she could now live with the thought of dying the violent death that she did. It was the *kaddish* which had helped her with this acceptance, and she wanted to thank me for it.

Ever since then, whenever I say *kaddish* for anyone, I think of it as a very special blessing. And even though I know that it's not really a "prayer for the dead" because it makes no mention of death, I also know that it really is some sort of vehicle, whereby the dead can find peace, even after a violent and horrendous death. Therefore, I hope that when I go, I will have a *kaddish,* because to a Jewish soul, this is a very important thing.

> *Magnified and sanctified be the Name of G-d throughout the universe which He has created according to His Will . . .*
>
> *May G-d's Great Name be praised for ever and ever . . .*
>
> *May there be abundant peace from heaven, and life for us and all the people Israel, and let us say "Amen."*
>
> *May the One Who creates peace in the heavens above, give peace to us and to Israel [and to the whole world]. Amen.*
>
> [excerpts from the *Kaddish*)

Chapter 9:

I Remember

by Carole Louie

I sit quietly in the healing circle at meditation, where, indeed, my own healing began. For years I searched for understanding and answers about why horrible things had happened to me. I felt gentle in my heart—why, then, did I have to suffer such pain? Why would anyone have to suffer? The answer now rings in my ear like a temple bell: "It's all about love. It's all about love . . . "

The door to my healing process first opened when my father died in 1990. I watched as his coffin lay in the earth and wondered if I would now be released from the painful memories that we shared. His death also made me question my own beliefs about life on the other side.

I am Amerasian. At my father's Chinese Buddhist wake and funeral, I decided to document the story of the rituals, as a legacy for my family. Although I already knew many of the rituals, I did not truly understand their meanings. As I asked and researched about the Buddhist customs, I also learned that ritual in general is taken too much for granted. In reality, ritual contains many important teachings; through learning about my father's funeral, I also discovered the purpose and meaning of reincarnation.

Long after my father's funeral, I was still haunted by memories of being molested by him and how that had changed my life. When I began to write the story of my father's funeral, something awakened within me. At first, I wrote it just to get the memories out of my mind, as if writing them on a piece of paper would release them from inside me. Remembering the incident of abuse was the first of many layers of memories—from this life and past lives—that I would eventually remember.

I began to study meditation—and the real healing process began. Through meditation, I learned how to relax and become more centered, grounded, and focused. This was a very important part of the process for me. Like so many people who first begin to meditate, I had a difficult time getting my body and mind to be quiet. But I soon learned and was then able to release the stress from my everyday life. As I became more centered and grounded, I also learned how to listen to the small voice within me. It was not like the mental chatter that goes on in our minds when we are busy doing this and that. It was a loving, comforting voice that seemed to be guiding me. So I listened.

One thing led to another as my psychic abilities awakened. Soon I was deep into the study of metaphysics. By using past-life regression techniques, I was eventually reunited with my father in two previous incarnations, also in abusive situations. I began to understand that my father and I chose to come back together again, as an opportunity to clear up our negative karmic energy.

At first, I resisted the idea that I was responsible for choosing my experiences, until I realized that if I did indeed choose them, then I could also choose to undo them. Furthermore, I could choose to create something much better than what I had created before. After that, I began to feel differently about my father. I found a great sense of forgiveness and compassion, as I viewed all of our lives together from a soul level, with detachment and unconditional love.

Yet in spite of all those months of meditation, research, and practicing, I still was not prepared for the moment when my father's spirit came to me in the healing circle during meditation. He felt like a ghost. He felt very cold when he was around me. At first I was afraid, but I worked through my fear. He asked me to forgive him. He explained that he was stuck in the earth plane because we had not resolved our issues before his death.

I wanted my father to be happy, so I did what he asked of me. Because he was Buddhist, I created a Buddhist ritual to release his spirit to heaven. I myself did not practice Buddhist ritual, but I knew it was important to honor his belief. So I performed the ritual. And ever since that time, I have been free of the pain that was caused by my father's molesting me.

Further research and journeying through time guided me in the cause and effect of events and circumstances in many lifetimes. My work gave me a better understanding of how and why I created everything in my present life.

At first, the memories came in my dreams. Then something during the day would trigger a déjà-vu feeling about the dream. I realized that certain physical pains were triggers for past-life memories. Words, phrases, actions, sounds, smells, and tastes would shock me with a memory that flashed across my mind. During meditation, visions also came to me. Somehow I knew they were connected to the memories in my dreams, so I began to keep a journal of them. From my notes, I then researched the meaning of my visions.

In addition, I desperately wanted to talk to someone who would understand what I was going through. I knew I wanted someone who understood the spiritual path and metaphysics, so I prayed to find such a person. Quite miraculously, I found Dr. Brian Weiss, author of *Many Lives, Many Masters* and *Through Time into Healing*. I devoured his books and attended two workshops. At the same time, I also made contact with Arthur Cataldo, a hypnotherapist who specializes in past-life regression. Lacking the financial resources to go to Weiss or Cataldo on a regular basis, I worked on my own with Cataldo's guided imagery techniques, until I could "journey-at-will" (through self-hypnosis) into a memory as it was being triggered.

When a painful feeling or memory seemed to come from nowhere, I centered myself, focused on it with love, then listened and watched. Sometimes the information was instantaneous. Sometimes it was like watching a movie. Sometimes I felt emotions without any knowledge of their source. Altogether, it was like a giant jigsaw puzzle: colorful, diverse, mysterious. At times it was also hell for me and for those around me. In the end, the various past lives that I reviewed ultimately brought me to the memory of my incarnation just prior to this one—as Anna Maria, a young Jewish girl who died in the Holocaust.

All of my life, I have been somewhat aware of a Jewish past-life connection. As I progressed in my spiritual work, I began to understand exactly what that connection was. In 1992, I watched a public television program about the meanings of the ritual for the Jewish Passover celebration. I was amazed at so many similarities between Jewish Passover and Christian Easter rituals.[1] I resonated strongly with what I learned from this program. In what life, I wondered, had I been Jewish?

Then in 1993, I was invited to celebrate the Passover Seder with a Jewish family. They went through the motions, but it was obvious that the rituals held little meaning for them. I was glad when they asked me to read a section of the ceremony, and I truly felt it in my heart and soul. Again I wondered: In what other life or lives had I been Jewish?

After that, the memories began to flood my consciousness. I remembered 1942. I remembered France. I remembered World War II . . . In bits and pieces the memories came back, until, at last, the puzzle was completed, and I knew myself as Anna Maria:

> I remembered my mama, with her warm arms wrapped around me and her heartbeat beneath her soft, full breasts. On many nights in that life, her embrace was all I had to keep me warm. I remembered how she gently rocked and rocked me, to comfort me against the misery that we now faced. I wondered what had happened to our beautiful home as I now huddled in Mama's arms in our corner of this dismal attic. Yet I also gave thanks that we had this dismal place to huddle in. And I gave thanks for the people who sheltered us from the oppressive Nazis.
>
> Over and over I wondered, "How can people treat other people in this way?" But I am only a child. What do I know? "Mama, please rock me, hold me, and help me release this pain . . . "
>
> I remember the night Papa did not come home. I stayed awake all night worrying about him. Another day passed and another night and then five more days. I could hardly sleep during that time, as I lis-

tened to every sound, waiting to hear his familiar footsteps up the stairwell.

I cried. I was so afraid of what might have happened to Papa. Each day, the fear and worry grew worse. I tried to believe he would come back, but each day that he did not, my fears grew. Finally, I could stand it no more. I curled up in my little bed, trying desperately to stay warm, trying desperately not to think about food . . .

I slept and dreamt of walking with my papa on the mountain slopes in springtime. It was a beautiful sunshiny day. The air was filled with the smell of new grass and the flowers that were bursting forth everywhere in radiant colors. I held my papa's hand and felt his love in his smile and in his eyes . . .

A noise overhead broke into my dream, and I listened as the hum of planes foreshadowed yet another air raid. We huddled in our makeshift shelter, praying that we would be spared in this assault. Perhaps it was being awakened so suddenly, or the lack of sleep, or the condition of my body, or the fear that had been building up inside of me—but I suddenly felt as if I must know where my papa was. I was cold. I was rocking and rocking, trying to be warm but I was so thin and it was so cold. "Papa, Papa, where are you?" my soul cried out.

Then I must have fainted or collapsed as my soul followed a beam of light, which told me that my papa was still alive. I traveled on this beam of light and suddenly found myself standing next to my papa. I tried to touch his hand—and that was when I knew he did not see me. "Papa, Papa! It's me, Anna Maria! Please talk to me, Papa."

His face was like a ghost. His body was limp and lifeless. He moved so slowly, step by step. All of the men around him moved this way, too. I saw their bodies shriveled up and I felt their souls were shriveled up, too, within their bodies. No one would talk to me. No one would listen. Step by step, I walked with them. It took so much effort to make each step.

One by one, each man was herded into a sterile room. I did not know what to do and so I waited, hoping that at any moment Papa would recognize me. It seemed as if we were separated by an invisible veil. And then the doors closed and I heard the sound of the bolt going across the doors. Silently the men and my papa stood waiting for the next thing to happen. I heard the noise as the air began to change. I smelled the gas and watched helplessly as everyone gasped for life. There was no life left in them so they merely succumbed to death.

I looked around at the heap of bodies on the floor. I heard my papa say to me, "What could we do? Anna, somehow you must survive this, and you must go out and tell the others. Now, I must go and meet my God." For an instant he reached out to touch my hand. Then he was gone.

I stayed with my father's body even though I knew he was no longer there. I watched as other souls lifted out of the heap of bodies and drifted to the beam of light overhead. Slowly at first, but then very quickly, they all left—and I sat alone with the heap of skin and bones, the smell of sweat, and urine, and gas.

Then the bolt slid across the door again, letting in another, more earthly light. Uniformed creatures picked up the bodies and threw them onto an open cart. I should not have stayed any longer, but I had to. I was only a child, but somehow I felt as if I must say something as these bodies were to be buried.

The large pit that had been prepared was now heaped with bodies until they were higher than the edge of the pit. Gasoline was poured over the bodies, and they quickly caught fire. I watched as the flames rose up and smoke filled the sky overhead, and when I knew I could not take it any longer, I said, "God go between me and thee, 'til we are one with each other." That was all I knew to say.

I must have slept for a long, long time in the attic, because when I woke up, I was so stiff—but it was warmer now. I did not know where I was at first. Then I heard my mama humming, but I was in a catatonic state. I could not speak. I could barely eat. I slept most of the time and when I wasn't sleeping, I was in a daze. I don't know what I did or how I did it, I only remember Mama's humming . . .

I never fully recovered from this state. Therefore, I never heard the sound on the stairwell. I only remembered Mama's startled reaction as loud sounds invaded our solitude. It happened so quickly. Fear rose up in me, as I saw men in the same uniforms that had been responsible for my papa's death—but still I could not speak. I clung to Mama's skirt as two SS men pulled her away from me, and in that instant I knew that I would never see my mama again. I shuddered and cried out, "Mama, don't leave me!"

Then I felt a fat strong hand on my wrist and at the instant of his grasp I could feel the ill intention and I could see my life pass before me. I would have run away but I was too weak and he was too strong. I could hear him say, "I like little girls," but all I could feel was evil in his words. I could feel his strong desire to relieve himself, and I knew that my body would be used for that purpose.

It happened quickly. He grabbed me and threw

me on the table, and the next thing I felt was his throbbing motions and my flesh ripping as he sodomized me. Fearing I would cry out, he cupped his hand over my mouth, and in his moment of relief he grabbed my neck as I gladly let go of my last breath. "How odd"—I thought in the next moment, "How odd to watch him hold my lifeless body and call me Liebchen." At that moment, I felt a sense of pain for him, greater than what I felt for my lifeless body. I did not feel the cold anymore nor the hunger, nor the fear . . .

And then I was embraced by the light. I felt more love and peace and joy than I could ever remember. But even in this state of peace, I vowed to keep my father's last wish to tell the others. I heard this vow echo back to me, and knew I must not waste any time . . .

The story is now told to fulfill that past-life vow.

* * *

In 1947, only five earthly years after Anna Maria's death in France, I was born as Carole in America. I brought with me the memories of Anna Maria, but it has taken me forty-seven years to consciously remember. At times, it was very confusing to know that I could "see" things not related to my present reality. And yet, allowing my consciousness to remember the memories of Anna Maria and to clear my karmic energy of them has been a liberating experience.

At last I could make sense out of my fear about enclosed staircases that lead to attics or the nausea I would feel whenever I smelled gasoline. I knew the reason I would rock myself whenever I was sad or afraid, and the pain that I felt when I saw other people being mistreated and abused. I now understood my love of Jewish culture and the way the word "Papa" sang to my heart, even though neither of these things were part of my upbringing.

In the summer of 1995, I traveled to France. I thought, almost with a sense of fear, that being in France would bring up the déjà-vu memories of Anna Maria. And yes, there were some of those feelings, as I walked in the pastures of the dairy farms on the mountain slopes in the French Alps. I had some strange moments, when I felt a sense of sadness, which I could not begin to discuss with my traveling companions. But most of my sensations of France were more connected with the French people and their love of life.

However, the true purpose of my trip to France was not to relive old memories. It was to go to Plum Village[2] and know my Dharma. At Plum Village, I sat with the Zen master, Thich Nhat Hanh. There I felt so much love that it filled my vessel to overflowing. I was finally at peace with the healing process, which started with my father's death, then took me on a journey through time, and now brought me back to France and fully into the present. At Plum Village, I rejoiced in the Buddhist rituals to celebrate life.

Through struggling with understanding the cause and effect of the Holocaust, I have also come to understand the power of the Collective Consciousness. I believe that years of man's abusive treatment toward his fellow man created such times as the Holocaust. The Holocaust was not only about abusers, but also about allowing abuse. To love one's self enough not to allow one's self to be abused is just as important as not to abuse others. And little abuses, left unresolved, create karmic opportunities to repeat abusive situations. Therefore, we need to be conscious of all the subtle variations of how we treat each other and clear the karmic energy so that the cycles do not repeat.

I now know peace that is indescribable, and I know what it truly means to love. I also know joy and the beauty of life. And I have come to believe, with all my heart and soul, that just as Collective Consciousness once created a Holocaust, so can it also create a world of peace. "Let there be peace on earth, and let it begin with me . . . "

Chapter 10:

To Triumph over Evil

by Linda Thieman

Each of us is born into this world in a state of what I call "unhealedness." I believe that it is the natural inclination of the human soul to grow toward greater healing. But, as part of the healing path, there must always be a period of grieving for any loss, whether in this lifetime or another lifetime. We grieve for what was, and we grieve for what might have been. We grieve for our own pain and for that of others. And then we learn to forgive.

Throughout my life, there have been many echoes from a previous incarnation in Nazi-infested Europe—a past life that I did not know existed until adulthood. Yet, looking back, there were many clues. At the age of twelve, I devoured Shirer's historical classic, *The Rise and Fall of the Third Reich.* During my teens, I sat glued to the television, watching *Hogan's Heroes,* a sitcom about American soldiers outwitting buffoonish Nazis in a German P.O.W. camp. *Hogan's Heroes* was meant to be humorous, but I always watched with a knot in my gut.

At age eighteen, I viewed *Night and Fog,* the concentration camp footage that was shot by the Nazis themselves. Seeing this horrifying footage launched me into a downward spiral that resulted in a profound depression which lasted for many months. I found myself racked with "survivor's guilt," even though the war was over before I was even born. Still, agonizing questions circled round and round in my head: Why hadn't I done more to help? Why was I trapped in powerlessness now? What could I have done? How could I help now?

Not until the age of thirty-one did I find the answers . . .

* * *

After I graduated from college in 1980, I spent a year living in Strasbourg, France. There I met my first husband, an Armenian Christian from Iran. We returned to the United States, got married, and both went back to college. Eventually I earned a master's degree in teaching English to speakers of other languages.

The first couple of years of our marriage worked well. We studied and had part-time jobs. But after we graduated, we faced a period of unemployment. My husband, a kind and decent man, was home less and less, as he became obsessed with business schemes. Soon he was spending all of his time with his Iranian friends, trying to make something work. His relatives in Kuwait told him that, if we moved there, they would find him a job. Eventually I found a position teaching English at Kuwait University, and we were off to the Middle East.

Our marriage did not improve in Kuwait. My husband's relatives reneged on their promise to find him work, and I ended up supporting both of us. Meanwhile, my husband spent all of his time at his relatives' homes, eating every meal with them, in the hope that somehow a business contact would appear.[1] After three years of trying everything I could think of to regain my husband's interest in me and our marriage, I finally gave up, defeated and depressed.

A pain-ridden divorce followed. My social network was ripped from me. As my soon-to-be-ex-husband returned to the States, his oldest cousin withdrew her support, and my best friend in Kuwait moved to Spain. I was left alone and friendless in that dry, barren desert that reflected the state of my soul.

During this stressful period of my life, I was consoled by a young Palestinian man whom I had met in 1984 at the birthday party of another teacher at Kuwait University. Looking back, I now see that this meeting was one of those "instant recognition" encounters between people who knew each other in a previous incarnation. Today, that type of reaction would sound warning alarms in my head. Back then, I had no idea that it meant anything at all.

After that "chance" meeting, this young man called to chat with me every three months or so. I thought it was because he had a talent for English and liked to practice speaking with the American teachers. But my husband thought differently. According to Middle Eastern custom, it was inappropriate for me to associate with a man who was not my husband. So I respected my husband's wishes and did not see the young Palestinian socially.

Shortly after my husband returned to the States to file for divorce, the Palestinian made his usual phone call. I told him what had been happening during the past year in Kuwait, and he helped me to pick up the shattered pieces of my life. If we had left it at that—if I had been strong enough to accept the healing that he offered and then go my own way—then we would have completed a karmic cycle that had gone on for several lifetimes. But I was neither that wise nor that strong, nor did I have any awareness of reincarnation or karma. In effect, I was operating blind.

After I moved back to the States, my relationship with the Palestinian quickly developed into a rebound marriage. My new husband's personality seemed to change overnight. Where once he had soothed my pain, now he only created more. He became abusive towards me, emotionally, psychologically, and physically. I ended up struggling for years to free myself from my entanglement with this man.

Our situation was further complicated by the fact that in 1988 I had accepted a teaching position in Japan. Because the Japanese courts did not have any jurisdiction over our marriage, we could not divorce there. At the time, this was very frustrating for me, but I now believe that it was meant for me to remain in this relationship until I learned how to forgive.

In March of 1990, while we were still in Japan, I had my first spontaneous memory of a past life during World War II. Soon after that, I was able to call up more memories through guided meditations and began writing down what I could "see." The more I wrote, the more the details came through to me.

From these memories, I learned that I was once a Jewish woman living in the outskirts of Paris. One day, a young SS officer arrived at my door and took my husband away. We were among the last Jews left in France at that time, because my husband was active in the underground, helping other Jews to escape. When we had our own chance to leave, my husband had refused to go, and I would not leave him behind. Now it was too late.

Although the young SS officer and I had never met before, when I opened the door to him on that bleak day, there was a look of startled recognition on his face. At the time, neither of us understood the source of this reaction. Nevertheless, that look of recognition set off a chain of events that not only changed his life and mine, but carried over into our current incarnations as well—*the soul that was the Nazi officer became my Palestinian husband.*

Only now—in this life—do I realize that I had known this same soul from yet another incarnation, during the so-called glory days of the Roman Empire. In that life, he had been a Roman soldier, and I was his female slave. I was Jewish in that life, too. As my master, he had treated me gently in bed, but still despised the fact that I was Jewish.[2] Then as now, it was a very tormented relationship.

During World War II, my old Roman master had returned as the SS officer who, once again, had power over my life and death. And yet, in spite of his position of authority, he was young and very inexperienced in the ugliness of war. Because of his flair for the French language, he had recently been posted to this plum assignment in Paris, but had never actually gotten his hands dirty. Now the combination of "recognizing" me and of sending my husband to his death engulfed this young German officer in guilt and shame.

The next afternoon, he came to warn me that I would be arrested next. The warning came as no big surprise, because I had already begun to feel that there was something to that look of recognition from the day before. Exactly what, I did not know.

I had to make a choice. Although I had had an escape plan prepared, it was now too late to use it. Only through the help of this SS officer would I be able to survive the war, by passing for a Christian. It was a matter of life or death. I chose life, but then had to live with the shame of my association with the Nazi officer until my death as the French woman in 1956. While I had been passing for

Gentile, the Jews around me perished. I felt as if I had abandoned my people in order to save only myself.

Recalling these past-life memories helped me to pinpoint the cause of my inexplicable "survivor's guilt" in this life. Just knowing that it was survivor's guilt—a common psychological phenomenon among people who have lived through a devastating catastrophe—has helped me to deal with the residual pain.

I also learned that, as the French woman, I had indirectly done a great deal for the Jews in Paris. Although I was not in the underground, I was heavily involved in a barter network. Bad times in general, and even worse times for Jews, had caused extreme shortages of food, clothing, and other supplies. Once I remembered that I had organized the exchange of goods and services from family to family, my guilt began to subside.

At the time of my psychic breakthrough in 1990, I began to meet other people that I had known in my past life as a French Jew. One of my former students was a rabbi who died during the war and is now Japanese. I also met the man who had been my Jewish father during the French life. In that incarnation he died when I, as the French Jew, was still young, and was reborn into his present life as an American in 1926. He came back as a "WASP" with a feel for things Jewish, just like I did.

Meeting these people again in this life filled me with such joy that I learned to recognize that joy as a signal that past-life memories about these people were coming my way. But not all of my psychic impressions were so pleasant. I also met a man who had been a Nazi in his former life and was still cruel in this one. When I realized this, I actively despised him, both for what he had been and what he was now. At the same time, I was deeply disturbed by my feelings of profound hatred toward this man. In learning to cope with my own past life during

World War II, I had already done a great deal of grieving and healing, and had begun to find a measure of inner peace. Now this unpleasant encounter had come along and upset my equilibrium again.

When one is confronted with something as immensely evil as the reign of the Nazis, it requires unrelenting effort to grieve over the losses and even more effort to learn to forgive. I struggled with this issue for a very long time. One thing which helped me enormously was the book *Life Between Life* by Dr. Joel Whitton and Joe Fisher,[3] which contains case studies of people who can remember the "interlife" state between incarnations. After reading about the interlife, the most compelling realization finally hit me: before we are born into a new human life, each of us has a plan. The plan for the next lifetime is devised with the help of high, loving spiritual beings and is meant to be positive and uplifting. The goal, as we see it during the interlife, is never revenge and cruelty, but to make amends and achieve some measure of healing.

I now believe that each person comes to earth with this intention to heal. But once we are born, the veil of forgetfulness blocks our vision, and we get caught up in the "density" of the earth plane. For some of us, that veil is so thick that we forget to look within for our true knowledge of God. Instead, we focus on what we can get from others. The original intent of our lives on earth is lost in the mist of time, memory, and incarnation into a new body. But what gives me the hope to go on is the realization that, no matter how entangled we might be in our earthly existence, the original intention for healing is still there.

So why, I asked myself, did these particular people come into my life, where they caused me so much pain?

After many years of contemplating this question, I

have come to believe that people who commit unspeakable acts of cruelty have little awareness about how the universe works on the spiritual level. To them, the idea of God is separate from life on earth—something to be believed in or not, with no integration of God into their daily lives. It is as if such people are trapped in a cold, dark, steel cage, lost and alone, desensitized to the process through which choices are made and to the consequences of their actions. Their decisions do not come from a place of calm centeredness, but from a place of anger, fear, and pain.

Once I chose to believe that each of us is doing the best we know how, to find our way back to God, then I began to let go of the pain caused by the Nazis. I could see that there is a "spectrum of healedness" to our existence, which is individualized, according to each person's level of awareness. On one end of this spectrum is wholeness and infinite awareness of God. On the other end is stuffed-down pain and anger and complete unawareness of God.

During my meditations, I learned that the SS officer, when he reached the afterlife, had come to deeply regret his responsiblity for my husband's death during the 1940s. So, he had chosen to return again, as the Palestinian from Kuwait, in order to make it up to me by helping me through the loss of my husband in this life. Had we simply remained friends, he would have succeeded. But the rebound marriage began another cycle of karma, which, in turn, required its own grieving and healing.

The awareness of these things eventually led to my letting go of judgment. Once I was able to put some time and distance between myself and my second husband, I could see his behavior as a symptom of the degree to which he was unhealed. I came to believe that to judge a certain behavior as "evil" only reinforces that behavior on an "energy level" and holds it in place on the wheel of karma. On the other hand, to acknowledge that every person on the face of the earth is here for healing—even if his or her actions seem unspeakably evil to us—is to be able to forgive and triumph over that very evil.

My own forgiveness finally came when I realized that I *had survived*—not beaten and forlorn, but strengthened and enriched. The painful circumstances I had lived through had led directly to my own spiritual awakening, which, in turn, had kindled the passion for spiritual growth that has blossomed into a lifelong commitment. By rising like a phoenix from the ashes of destruction and despair, I not only released myself from the prison of my own hurt, but also helped the people who had hurt me. On the level of spiritual energy, I released the karmic ties between us, so that they, too, can make faster leaps in their own healing process.

* * *

But that's not the end of the story. In the spring of 1993, while still in Japan, I discovered Rabbi Gershom's book, *Beyond the Ashes*. The book had a profound effect on me because it gave me a much wider context for some of the things I was going through. So I wrote to the rabbi with my story, and he wrote back. This correspondence, which grew into a friendship, has helped me deal with my conflicting feelings about my identity.

After my death as the French Jew in 1956, I was reborn into a German-American Protestant family in 1958. At the age of sixteen, I threw off the Christian belief system in which I had been reared, but continued to "pass" for a Christian within the family circle. Not until 1992 did I finally find the courage to tell my mother that I am not Christian.

For much of my adult life, I felt like a "secret Jew," but tried to deny these feelings because the body I wear now is not Jewish. Yet there is something of my Jewish past lives which still comes through. Of the handful of Jews that I have known in this life, three have asked me if I am Jewish, as if they somehow sensed my Jewish soul. Interestingly, not one single non-Jew has ever asked me that.

For a long time, I struggled with this inner conflict between my past and present lives. Rabbi Gershom's acceptance of me as a "Jewish soul in a Gentile body" has helped me deal with this odd identity crisis. I used to feel like I was denying who I really was, although neither "Jew" nor "Gentile" really seemed to fit. Finally, I just decided to accept myself the way I am, an integration of both.

About the same time that I read the rabbi's book, while I was still in Japan, I also began to attract many "ghosts" or earthbound spirits. Prior to this, I had never had much interest in ghosts. These spirits both frightened and annoyed me. They surrounded me from a distance, looking lost and forlorn. At night when things were quiet, I was aware of so many spirits that they seriously disturbed my sleep—so much so that I sometimes had to sleep in the daytime to avoid them.

Looking back, I now believe that many of these spirits were earthbound Holocaust victims who had attached themselves to me when I visited the site of a concentration camp in the hills of eastern France back in 1980. They had continued to follow me around without my knowledge for all those years, but I did not become aware of them until after my own past-life memories surfaced. At the time, I had no understanding of how earthbound spirits can attach themselves to living people, nor did I know how to send them "into the light."

A week after receiving Rabbi Gershom's answer to my first letter (on the night of October 23, 1993, to be exact), I was feeling really suffocated by all of these ghosts. As I tossed and turned in bed, there were so many ghosts around that I literally could not breathe. Then suddenly, I became aware of the spirits of Hasidic men in the room with me, and I thought to myself, "There must be nine or ten Hasidim in my room!" As soon as I thought that, I knew they were a *minyan* (Jewish prayer quorum.)[4]

At first I was really annoyed—here were more spirits, coming to crowd me out of my home! But within two days, the whole house was cleared of ghosts, except for the *minyan* of Hasidim. I then realized that they were an answer to a prayer. These Hasidic spirits had come to help me take another step forward, to protect me, and to complete a cycle of healing for the earthbound spirits, which I did not have the power to do on my own.

Once I got over my initial annoyance at their presence, I welcomed the Hasidim as teachers. The *minyan* remained with me for one month, until their work was done. When it was time for them to move on, they did so gradually, in stages. They would move further away in my consciousness, remain there for a while, and then move further on. Today, they are like a tiny, distant point of light in my awareness. Still, if I ever need to call on them again, I know that they will be there for me.

Today, my dedication to my spiritual path is as strong as ever. I try to be very conscious of the choices I make and the consequences of each action. My psychic abilities continue to unfold. I now do spiritual readings for people in my local area and have begun to write about healing on the physical, emotional, and spiritual levels. In my daily life, I persist in working toward forgiveness when people hurt me. This is never easy, but it is rewarding. Although my understanding of the nature of God and spirituality continues to evolve, one thing does not change—I will always believe that forgiveness is necessary in order to triumph over evil.

Chapter 11:

My Little Precious

by "Rebecca"

I am an Australian Jew, born in 1953. My sister and I were brought up in a nonobservant home, where even discussing our Jewishness in public "too loudly" was frowned upon and seriously discouraged. So, of course, I did not grow up knowing about Jewish mysticism, nor did I know that Jews can believe in reincarnation.

Today, I live in Sydney with my husband and our children, each of whom brings a universe of knowledge with them. However, my relationship with one of my children, my ten-year-old daughter Leah,[1] has never flowed as easily as I would have liked. There have been times when she has looked at me with such intense hatred that I would fly into an old pattern of resentment, saying things that I would regret as soon as they were out of my mouth. The story I am about to tell is about the past-life relationship between Leah and me, and the karmic healing between us.

I have been studying spiritual healing for quite some time, and I now work as a past-life therapist. In 1994, I decided to make my own spiritual clearing and cleansing a top priority in my life. I gave up my job and, although I had no idea what the next day would bring, I simply knew that I was being guided, and trusted that whatever happened would be right for me. One thing led to another, until, one afternoon in January 1995, I decided to meditate on my karmic connection with my daughter Leah. This is what I saw:

> I am standing in green slime. I am about seven years old. It is slippery, and in my hand I am holding a bucket. There is a thin pipe protruding from the side of a building, and I am trying to fill the bucket with as much water as I can.
>
> A woman in dark clothing approaches me. She is huge and fat and is wearing black boots. She kicks the bucket out of my hands and screams to me to return to the "barracks" (this is the word I seemed to understand). She says I must run or she will kill me. There is hatred and fear in her face. I run and push open the door.
>
> I am hit with the smell of bodies. The beds are in three levels, one on top of the other. (Not two levels, as I have always imagined them to have been.[2]) I see women with no hair and huge hollow eyes. It is quiet in there, and I hide on the floor at the far end of the room, under the bunks. I begin to feel a dripping of something on my shoulder. It makes me feel incredibly cold. I crawl out and see my brother being born.
>
> He is born in total silence. The emptiness and desolation in the room is almost palpable. As this child slips into the world, the officer that I saw outside comes in and smells something. She comes over and my mother dies. The officer picks up the

baby and is about to kill it. There is fear and anger in this woman. I can't stand it and begin to scream. The scream is both in this life and that one. Then I hear the clearest voice saying, "Change it!"

The officer takes the baby away. I knew he would be all right. The next thing I saw was the baby being pushed into the room in an old box. The officer is leaving the camp in secret. I hold the baby and find that I am walking with a group of very sick people. I know I am going to die.

We are led into a large room. It seems to be tiled. I sit in the corner of the room and watch more and more naked people come into the room. I see holes in the walls and hear a hissing noise. I watch my brother turn blue and I hold my breath, but I die with everyone else. (I wonder: is the asthma I have in this life connected to that?) I am then greeted [in the spirit] by my mother from that life, who tells me that I shall never have another life like that. Then she guides me away.

The officer is my daughter Leah in this life.

I was deeply disturbed by the imagery of this meditation, and by the idea that my daughter might have been a Nazi in another life. So I decided to let the experience sink in before I told anyone. As I went about my business that day, I kept having a very strong feeling about that scene. I kept feeling that the officer was Jewish and had somehow made the army believe she was a German. Could this really have been true? I had never heard of such a thing.

Three days later, I was out shopping with my sister, and we noticed a parking spot outside Adyar, the biggest esoteric bookstore in Sydney. So I suggested that we go inside and have a look around. My sister found a number of wonderful books on Judaism. I just wandered around, happy to be there, browsing through this book and that . . .

I felt a bit tired and noticed a section on dreams, so I went over and picked up a book called *Dream Lovers* by Denise Lynn. I have been a student of Denise Lynn's and I love her work, so I thought to myself, "Oh good, so that's why I came here." My sister came over and we sat down on the floor between the shelves of books.

Just at that moment, as I was thinking that I should tell her about my past-life experience, I noticed, directly in front of me, a copy of *Beyond the Ashes* by Rabbi Gershom. There was only one copy of the book, and I had heard of this book from a friend in January that same year. Now I took it off the shelf and just stared at it. It seemed as if the book had found me, because although I had wanted to read it, I was not specifically looking for it at the time.

After reading the rabbi's book on Holocaust reincarnation cases, I wrote to him concerning my story about Leah and raised the question about whether or not a Jew could have posed as a German guard. The rabbi wrote back:

> Yes, that is certainly possible, and it did happen. The Germans defined a Jew as anyone who had one Jewish grandparent—either side of the family—so there were some who could "pass" for German if nobody knew about their family. There were also "Aryan-looking" Jews who got false identity cards and passed for Germans. Some did this to smuggle food, etc., but others got trapped in the role—once the deception was started, it was death to be found out . . .
>
> There were also some Jews who openly collabo-

rated with the Nazis in the camps. The "kapos," as they were called, were Jewish guards who worked under the German guards. Unfortunately, the kapos were often just as cruel as their Nazi masters. It is hard for us today to understand how this could be. Apparently, in prison situations everywhere, there are always some people who are willing to sell out their principles and collaborate with their captors.

Either way, the story you describe is perfectly plausible from an historical point of view. If this is indeed the case, then perhaps Leah chose to come back as your child in order to reconnect with her own Jewishness, as well as heal the personal karma between you. You described your own family background as "nonobservant" and secretive about being Jewish, but that would be a "step up" for the soul that was Leah, if it had been passing completely for a German in the previous life. I personally do believe in the idea of "Jewish souls," that is, of souls that accepted the Covenant at Sinai for all incarnations. During the Holocaust, however, the tests were severe, and some people chose safety over Jewish pride. If any of this rings true for you, please let me know.

Not only did this information "ring true," it also brought about a healing between Leah and me. Now I could understand why she got so angry if I didn't insist that the children keep the rules in the house. For example, I have said that there is to be no TV in the mornings, but sometimes, when all the children are ready early, I give in and let them watch for a short while. This would make Leah so angry that she would insist they turn off the TV, just because it was a rule.

Seeing this behavior in the context of the rabbi's letter, I suddenly understood how, in Leah's past life, a broken rule probably meant death. So we talked about the importance of rules, and I explained that I really do understand how she must be frustrated when I change the rules without explaining to everyone first. Nowadays, I try not to make "rules" at all, but, rather, just deal with each situation on its own merit.

I decided to read the rabbi's letter to my husband, who was very interested. He is open to all possibilities and never puts down my beliefs. As we were reading the letter together, Leah walked into the room. I told her that I had written to a rabbi in America about a past life that I remembered, when I was in the Holocaust. She asked me to tell her about it. I answered that I didn't feel ready to share it with her yet, but that I was so glad that she chose to be born as my daughter in this life. I told her that I thought she was the bravest, most courageous person and that I loved having her as my daughter.

She looked up at me with her little arms around my waist and said, "Mummy, was I in the story, too?" I said yes, she was. She was quiet for a few seconds, then said very softly, "Mummy, I was on the other side, wasn't I?"

I couldn't speak. I just held her and whispered that she was "my little precious." She giggled and said that she loved to be called that, so I said it again and again, until we were both laughing and hugging.

That was the turning point in our relationship. The looks of fear and hatred are rarely seen now, but when they do appear, I no longer take them personally. In fact, they now reach into my heart and remind me that Leah is here as my Jewish daughter in this life. And for that, I honor and admire her. She is in the process of her own healing—as are we all—only now it is so much easier for me to understand her, having seen a little from where she came.

Today, I continue my work in counseling and psychology, and I wonder about the role that this story might play here in Australia. Because Leah is still a minor, we chose not to use our real names, to protect her privacy. But that doesn't really matter, because the healing is still there. I believe that the world is opening doors for more people to be of service to their fellow souls on Earth. The spark of light within our souls can be made to expand, and not only can, but *must* be shared. When the time comes for those who need us to find us, Leah and I will be there.

Chapter 12:

The Scapegoat

by David D. Johnson

Rabbi Gershom's book about reincarnation, *Beyond the Ashes,* probably saved my life. In April of 1993, just before I found that book, I was 112 pounds overweight and so deeply depressed that I literally lived on the couch in front of my TV. Most of the time, the slightest effort to do anything else was just too emotionally draining. I was diagnosed as a stage four depressive, which meant that I had suicidal tendencies. I was also suffering from a severe case of Post Traumatic Stress Disorder (PTSD).

I was born in 1950 in Wisconsin and grew up in the Midwest. My father was mostly German, my mother Norwegian. As a boy in a German-American family, I was expected to be tough and able to withstand whatever happened to me, but I could not. My biological mother was verbally abusive, calling me foul names in the most hateful way. By the age of four, I was completely terrified of her. My father drank a lot and had a temper.

The ironic thing is that this was a typical upbringing

among German families where I grew up.[1] Neither of my parents believe that they did anything wrong. But they did. They shamed me to the core of my being, and I didn't recover my self-esteem until decades later.

In 1969, just after President Nixon's ridiculous speech on Vietnam, I enlisted. In many ways, the army and Vietnam were simply an extension of my upbringing. It was the expected thing for a man to do. I was in 'Nam for a year, part of it in aerial combat support. There were no particularly traumatic experiences for me in the army, beyond the usual stress of combat and the emotional paralysis that I had brought with me from childhood. I served my country well and returned to the States.

In 1974, I married, and in 1976 we moved to the Twin Cities, where we have lived in the same house since 1981. As you can see, except for my stint in the army, I spent most of my life in the upper Midwest. Why, then, did I always feel like a stranger?

By 1986, I was deep in depression. My entire life was based on a fear of being trapped. The unhumor of this fear is that it masked a deeper problem, namely, the feeling that I was a "subhuman." Because of this secret feeling, I could never get close to people and had very few friends. I couldn't even play games, because to lose was to be exposed at my very core as a "subhuman." My emotional state continued to slide downhill. Eventually, I quit my job, became extremely overweight, and was increasingly isolated.

On that particular Thursday in 1993, I had gone to Unity Church in Golden Valley, Minnesota, to attend a session on the workings of the Holy Spirit. Arriving a little early, I decided to browse in the church bookstore. My eye fell on a copy of Rabbi Gershom's work, *Beyond the Ashes: Cases of Reincarnation from the Holocaust.* I immediately grabbed it off the shelf. I, too, believed that

I might have been a victim of the Nazi Holocaust in a past life. For years, when I would close my eyes, I would see many nondescript faces, all waiting for me to help them somehow. Right now, even as I write this, I can still feel those faces around me, waiting.

I am not Jewish in this life. I was raised German Lutheran and now belong to the Unity Church. Still, I often feel more like a mystic Jew than anything else. I especially have a connection to Nostradamus. Once, during my self-hypnosis work, I even came up with a name, Alain, that was somehow associated with him. As Alain, I saw Nostradamus, who was under threat to deny his Jewish heritage.[2] Was I his student or associate? I do not know. But in this life, when I was introduced to astrology, I learned it very quickly and was soon interpreting charts better than people with many years of experience.

On another occasion, also during self-hypnosis, I experienced a past life of great intellectual power, where I was carefully watched over by some kind of authority, in order to make sure that I did not spread my ideas. In that life, I was burned at the stake. The feelings connected with that memory are similar to the feelings I have when I experience memories of Jewish past lives. I don't really know or care if these "lives" are true in the objective sense, because the allegory always teaches me something about myself.

But even though I am a certified hypnotherapist with a very strong interest in reincarnation, I had never before heard of a book that connected this subject with the Holocaust. Now I was holding just such a book in my hand! I opened it randomly. There, in the middle of the page, was a description of how the Nazis had sometimes used diesel trucks for makeshift gas chambers:

> The next technological "advance" in this human-made hell was to use panel trucks with the exhaust pipes rerouted into the cargo area. Contrary to popular opinion, the Jews did not enter these death vans willingly. They often screamed and fought back, but were beaten into submission. Then the trucks were sealed and the engines started. When the screams stopped, the trucks were driven to the woods where the bodies were buried.[3]

My mind reeled with amazement at this strange coincidence. For years, I had had serious problems with diesel fumes. Only a few weeks before, while ice fishing on my favorite lake, I had suddenly become dizzy and nauseated. I soon figured out that I must be smelling diesel fumes from some trucks at a nearby construction site. I could clearly hear the truck engines running. But I was sitting on the ice, in the middle of the lake—so why had I reacted so strongly to trucks on the shore?

Even after I went home from the lake that day, the symptoms remained. In fact, the dizziness from that truck incident lasted five weeks, during which time I hallucinated and felt very sick and nauseous. And lately, this kind of physical reaction was getting to be an all-too-common occurrence in my life. Now, as I stood there in the church bookstore, I asked myself: Could this be something from a past life? So I bought the rabbi's book on Holocaust reincarnations and continued reading it until the class started.

The next day was Friday. It was an emotionally difficult day for me, not so much because of the book, but as a continuation of my ongoing spiral. I was so depressed that I called my sister, who works as an aide in the psych ward of a major hospital. She was extremely worried about my state of mind that day and wanted me to drive up to Minneapolis right away, to voluntarily check myself in for treatment. I reluctantly agreed, but asked if we could wait until Tuesday. I had found this book on reincarnation, I explained to her, which was causing strange reactions in my thinking, and I wanted to finish reading it first.

That same Friday, I read *Beyond the Ashes* from cover to cover—TWICE! The next day, on Saturday morning, I got up off the couch, went outside, and mowed the lawn. Not only that, but I actually enjoyed it—something that would have been impossible before, because of my panic attacks and depressive feelings. Now, for the first time in many years, I was really enjoying something! Strange as it may seem, that simple bit of yard work was a major breakthrough toward my full recovery.

Over the next few days, my emotional state improved rapidly. Two weeks later, I began an exercise program, which was a real first for me. Except for boot camp, I had never seriously exercised in my entire life, although I had played some tennis in college. Now I was determined to take off that extra 112 pounds of flab. But first, I had to deal with a very frustrating setback.

When I first began doing the exercises, the panic attacks and the depression returned. I definitely didn't want to go back to that negative cycle again! So I took some time off to go fishing, on the very same lake where I had heard the diesel trucks back in January. Of course, the construction was finished and the lake had thawed out, so I now fished from the shore. It was quiet and peaceful. I sat there in silence and just meditated.

Then the answer came to me. Whenever I did any kind of exercise, I was pumping adrenaline into my system. But my body was somehow confusing this natural chemistry with *fear!* Instead of giving me an "athlete's high," the adrenaline was triggering a panic attack. But why was I so afraid in the first place?

The fear seemed to be connected with my Holocaust past life somehow. Perhaps it was a remembrance of the Nazis or some other group terrorizing the Jews. Once I realized this connection, I was able to continue with the exercises, panic free!

Over the next year and a half, I lost seventy-two pounds. When I finally returned to work as an IBM mainframe computer consultant in 1994, I was in better shape, both physically and emotionally, than when I had quit two-and-a-half years before.

But the healing did not stop there. In November of 1994, I had signed up for a workshop on "Reincarnation and the Holocaust," which Rabbi Gershom was teaching at the Evenstar School[4] in St. Paul, Minnesota. I was very excited to finally be meeting him. But on the day before the class, I became so ill that I had to leave work early. The next day, too, I felt just awful and had to call in sick. I was very worried that I would still be sick that evening and was going to miss my chance to meet the man whose book had changed my life.

At the same time, I was also taking medication for an ear problem. As the day progressed, I figured out that the ear medication was somehow interacting with the caffeine in my coffee, causing my heart to pound extremely hard. There was that darned adrenaline problem again. This time, it forced me to examine another deep-seated issue.

As I explained above, all my life I had felt like a subhuman, not even worthy of being a second-class citizen. Back in April of 1993, when I first read *Beyond the Ashes,* I had come to understand how a helpless young Jew might have believed she really was subhuman, especially if she did not have enough support around her to know that the Nazis' ideas about "inferior races" were false. Rabbi Gershom explained how the Nazis had purposely desecrated the Jewish holy days, ceremonies, and ritual objects, in order to link "being Jewish" with humiliation. Under such circumstances, a child or teenager who did not have much life experience to fall back on might easily feel ashamed to be Jewish.

When I thought about my past life in the Holocaust, I somehow sensed that I had been an adolescent Jewish girl, between the ages of twelve and fifteen. Over the years, I have had many dreams in which I was a young girl. Now I also realized that I had carried internalized feelings of inferiority from that life into this one.

Whenever I meditate on this Holocaust life, the word which comes to mind is *fear.* I am still afraid to explore that life in detail, because it is so painful. But one thing I do understand now—that feeling of subhumanness is not my fault. I am free of it today, because I learned how the Nazis were playing with the Jewish minds. As that young Jewish girl, I had internalized their shame-based program. When I finally realized that the Nazis were game-playing with my self-esteem, my whole life changed again.

Because I was home sick anyway that day and because the rabbi's workshop was the same evening, I decided to reread the book. Partway through, I stopped and did a self-hypnosis exercise, focusing on the idea of the scapegoat.[5] I tried to visualize that part of me which felt subhuman and use the scapegoat archetype to understand my problem about feeling so inferior.

Under self-hypnosis, the scapegoat image appeared to me as a pinkish Caucasian monster, about half my height. His head was huge—three times the diameter of his body—and had outer grooves on it, something like a baseball. I understood this image to represent a part of myself, so I told this monster that I understood him and that I needed his strength to feel equal around other people. The monster replied several times, "You don't want me around!"

He didn't say this as a young child might do, hoping to hear me say, "Oh, yes, I really do want you," and be comforted. No, the monster really did believe that he, the scapegoat, wasn't good enough to be around even little old me!

Next, I tried to get in touch with that feeling of inferiority, and I was successful. As I sat there, I could see that the monster had stopped walking away from me. Then his head opened up. Out walked forty or fifty beings of golden light—*and they walked right into me!* From that moment on, I lost all feelings of subhumanness.

At Rabbi Gershom's workshop, I shared this story with other people who had past-life memories from the Holocaust. This was very healing for me and eventually led to my writing this essay. Over the next two months, I gradually let go of all the slights and pain associated with my internalized false shame.

No doubt, you are thinking that my recovery was now complete. But that wasn't the case at all. Instead, the healing process led to another major crisis. Because I had based my entire life on my feelings of subhumanness, when that was gone, I had *nothing left* to base my existence on. I was completely empty inside. Even my memory itself seemed to be failing me now, because my recall was somehow tied up with protecting myself from feeling like a subhuman.

At this point on my journey, I confided in my Unity minister, who genuinely understood my feelings. He suggested to me that it was time to pull back for a while and just rest from my ordeal. But, instead of taking his advice, I continued to dwell on it.

I felt worse and worse, until I finally reached a point

where I realized that, on the spiritual level, the part of me which had suffered was really an illusion. It—the personality who had experienced the suffering—was not the real me! It was only a projection of my Higher Self, the eternal soul that could never be harmed by others.

At the same time, on the level of the ego, I had indeed felt all of that pain. And now I felt cheated somehow. Perhaps my eternal soul had learned an important spiritual lesson, but it was at the expense of the "I" who had gone through it all. And now, that "I" seemed to be disappearing forever. I became very angry, because "David" had paid a very high price and in effect had been "used" by the eternal soul.

I experienced this feeling of anger very strongly for about one day. Then I also realized that the part of me which had suffered would never really die, because it is a part of my soul, too. I needed to have it come back into my Higher Self again, just as those shining beings had entered me, when I visualized the big-headed monster. Those beings were many lives, integrating into one.

What I learned in that vision was, that a strong negative experience stays with a soul, even over many lifetimes, but it becomes transformed into something positive. Those beautiful beings of golden light were other strong negative experiences, coming home to me. The golden beings were created over many lifetimes, and now at last they were able to come home. When my current hurting self—the incarnation that is David Johnson—realized this, I was cured!

So—am I me, or am I a girl in Nazi Germany? Of course, I am both, and more. Each personality is a part of the soul and will never die, ever. The mystical path is an incorporation of all our experiences. Yes, I suffered in my past lives and in this one as well, but I represent all that has gone before "me," in whatever form. I now feel that I have finished a major part of my path and can rest awhile, until God sees fit to have me serve in a new capacity.

EPILOGUE: On May 7, 1996, David wrote that he is totally free of depression and has "truly started a new life." He now walks or runs five miles per day, does hill climbing, and has given up most sweets and fattening foods. He is also continuing to pursue his metaphysical studies.

Chapter 13:

A Dream of Infinity

by Mary (Miriam) Marks

I was the fourth child born to a Gentile mother and a Jewish father in Los Angeles, California, in 1943. Even before my birth, my father had abandoned the family. I was left in the care of my mother and maternal grandmother, neither of whom knew anything about Judaism or Jews. My upbringing was strictly secular.

My early life was all about survival and hostility. Because of my father's desertion, my childhood was exceedingly harsh. The deprivations we endured caused my siblings and me to fight over everything from food to our mother's reluctant attention. An early bout of polio left me physically handicapped, and I received only sporadic medical care. There were times when we didn't have enough to eat and times when we were forced to share our house with rats. We were regularly evicted for not paying the rent, and my mother even indentured me to another family as a baby sitter when I was fourteen years old. In addition to all of this, I regularly endured sexual, physical, and emotional abuse from members of my family.

The frequent antagonism in our home caused me to turn inward. I had a strong sense of closeness to G-d[1] from my earliest years. At the age of two, I pondered the concept of infinity. When I was three years old, I dreamed that I was taken into the presence of G-d, where I heard the celestial *ofanim* (angels) singing praises to Him. I knew beyond a shadow of a doubt that G-d was real. Looking back, this was quite remarkable, since there was no real religion or talk of G-d in our home. How, then, could I have known about all this at the age of three?

The dream about G-d was not an isolated event. At various times in my life, I have had spiritually significant dreams that I knew came from G-d. When I was about ten years old, I twice had a recurring dream that was the same in every detail. Because this dream was about my own violent death, it frightened me as much as if it were a real event:

> The year is 1939 or 1940, somewhere in a big city in Europe or the United States—I can't tell which. I am a thirty-year-old, well-groomed woman. My slim good looks have served me well in this male-dominated Western culture. There is great social upheaval and death, and destruction is coming closer and closer. Until today, my attractiveness has inspired protection from the vile events occurring around me, but I intuitively know that everything in my life is about to change . . .
>
> I approach the building with anxiety and trepidation, feeling helpless against some nameless, impending betrayal. I smooth my jacket on my stylish gray wool suit, slightly adjust the hat on my short brown hair, square my shoulders, step into the elevator, press the button and ascend to the eighth floor.

The motors hum, the cables lift. After an express ride, a bell rings and the light goes on behind the number eight.

The elevator stops and the doors open. I seem to float from the elevator through the door to my doctor's office. He is bald, with just a fringe of closely cropped gray hair, clean shaven, and wears round, wire-rim glasses and a bland gray suit. I think he is a psychiatrist. He greets me soberly and I search his steely eyes for a clue—any clue—to my fate.

I am standing with my back to the door and facing the outside wall, which is lined with picture windows that are covered with horizontal wooden blinds with wide slats. The psychiatrist is standing in erect military posture to my left. In short, crisp statements, he makes it clear that he has done all he can for me. I don't understand specifically what is wrong, but something about me is unacceptable. Because of that, my life as I know it is about to change completely.

An adjoining door to my right opens from an office next door. Two more men walk into the room and stand in front of a dark bookcase in the corner. They are wearing dark suits, and one of them has a beard. The psychiatrist walks over to them, and the three men confer about what to do with me.

I am to be sent to a place where I will be a prisoner, completely controlled by others and doomed to spend the rest of my life in emotional and maybe physical pain. The prospect is terrifying. I begin to think that I would rather die than let them do that to me. Panic begins to rise in my breast, and my mind is racing, looking for a way to escape.

I am still facing the windows. I notice that one

blind is raised to admit a view of the city. It is nighttime, and the streets and huge stone office buildings are glistening with lights. Spreading infinitely above is a black, moonless sky, with millions of stars hanging against the sparkling black background. I slowly walk to the window, mesmerized by their beauty. The more I look at the stars, the more I see. Suddenly the world outside becomes a vast eternity filled with points of light that somehow beckon and inspire. I know what I must do.

The window yields and opens easily. I begin to climb out. The three men in the corner notice me and rush to stop me, but they are too late. I jump out the window to join myself with the darkness and the light.

During my descent, I am neither panicked nor afraid. I notice with some curiosity that the speed with which the air is rushing past me turns my skin very cold, and I begin to shiver. I did not expect that. Suddenly I hit the pavement below, and all the lights go out. There is no pain. I am dead.

The next thing I know, I am in a dark tunnel, traveling toward a light—but I do not want to go. I am aware that I have been dead for some time and that, in the interim, I have been "somewhere else." I also know that I have learned important information during that time, but suddenly I cannot remember what it was. It's as if a black veil has been deliberately drawn between me and that other place. But I do know that I was completely happy, loved, and fulfilled there, and I want with all my heart and soul to return.

I struggle, but my thoughts cannot penetrate the barrier.

I feel a momentum that is physically moving me

forward, through the tunnel and toward the light. "Don't make me go!" I scream in fear and despair, as the wonderful place recedes—but the movement is inexorable.

My fear takes over completely. I am screaming and crying as I emerge into a harsh, artificial light. There are very large people standing all around me, and it seems as if I am very small. I am screaming with terror, when all of a sudden I hear my own voice and realize that I am an infant.

I have just been born. The harsh light is the bright, round overhead lamp in the delivery room of a hospital, and the unbearable whiteness is light reflected off the sterile gowns of the doctors and nurses standing around me. I understand with growing despair that I cannot communicate my fear or the knowledge that I came from that other place. I notice that, with each scream, the past recedes and becomes more vague, while the present becomes a penetrating reality. I then realize that by the time I develop the ability to communicate, all knowledge of my past before birth will be lost.

In my infantile omnipotence, I think that everyone in the room—indeed in the whole world—has been created at the moment of my birth, solely for the purpose of playing a role in my life. I imagine that their existence is dependent upon mine and that they would not exist outside of my life. With deep melancholy I assume that I have entered an endless cycle of life, death, and rebirth—in which my life is destined to be painful and full of sorrows.

I do not want to enter this cycle again. I despair at the thought that, after thirty years, I will once more be compelled to commit suicide. Understandably, my wailing is inconsolable. My new name is Mary Marks. It is June 3, 1943, in White Memorial Hospital, Los Angeles, California. Already I have forgotten what my other name was.

I only had this dream twice, but it was exactly the same both times, and every detail was seared into my memory so that I would never forget. This dream about dying and being reborn contained information and symbols that I had no way of knowing at the age of ten—yet there they were. Where did this information come from?

During the next few years, I had one or two more spiritually significant dreams, but none as compelling or profound as that one. Then, when I was sixteen years old, I began to feel a strong imperative to be Jewish. I was the only one in my family to feel this way. When I tried to talk to my siblings about our Jewish father's heritage, they were uninterested.

In fact, I rarely saw my father, who had little influence in my life. Whenever I did mention my inclinations toward Judaism, he was completely disinterested. He spent his life running away from being Jewish. Oddly, it was my Gentile mother who encouraged me to be proud of my heritage, even though she did not realize what that entailed. She thought being Jewish was like being Irish or German—just another nationality.

During that same sixteenth year, I was living in a small town in northern California with my mother and younger brother. Compelled to start my spiritual odyssey, I went to the place most likely to inform me—the public library. I found only one book on the subject, Nathan Ausubel's thick history of the Jewish people. It was far too overwhelming. So I looked for Jewish names in the phone book. I knew only three for sure: Cohen, Marks, and Shapiro.

I found a Shapiro and called to see if there was a local

synagogue. I explained that I was sixteen, half Jewish, and interested in converting.[2] There was no formal synagogue in town, but she directed me to the local *minyan* (prayer quorum), which accepted me and took me in without question.

When I was with this tiny community, I felt that I had found my home at last. They taught me everything I could absorb in two short years. After that, I went to UCLA and joined the Hillel student association.[3] My Jewish education continued to the next logical step—a formal conversion. From then on, I lived as a Jew—first Reform, and later Conservative. But the rich intricacies of Orthodox Judaism and kabbalistic mysticism remained, for the most part, a complete mystery to me.

* * *

Because I knew only modern Judaism, which tends toward rationalism, I didn't dare take my dream seriously. After all, it was just a dream, wasn't it? For years it lay dormant in my memory, only occasionally rising to the surface to tease me with its suggestion of a past life.

Once, my Aunt Flora (on my father's side) said that she thought I was the reincarnation of her great-grandmother Malka, who had emigrated to Israel with her husband Nahum in 1898. There they had built a synagogue in Mea Shearim, the Orthodox section of Jerusalem. Our spirits were alike, she would tell me.

During my first visit to Israel in 1988, I made a pilgrimage to Tiferet Yerushalayim, Malka and Nahum's little shul in Jerusalem, where I touched the stone walls and thought, "Malka touched these." I made sure that her *Yahrzeit*—the anniversary of her death—was observed in the little yeshiva (religious academy) that they had founded a century before.[4] Tradition and connection to the past have always been very important to me, and remain so.

Shortly after that visit to Israel, the memory of the dream I had at age ten came flooding back. From that point on, I was compelled to find an interpretation. Over the years, I made several attempts to contact rabbis in Israel and the United States who might have the ability to interpret dreams, but each attempt failed. Then in 1993, I read Rabbi Gershom's book, *Beyond the Ashes,* and became so excited that I could hardly contain myself. Here, at last, was a way to understand so many things about my life. I had finally found a person who not only helped me interpret my dream, but also gave me a context for the suffering I had experienced since childhood.

* * *

The most important insights on the meaning of the dream came from a phone conversation with Rabbi Gershom, in which he suggested that I was supposed to go through the Holocaust in 1939, but chose to commit suicide instead. So, everything I had avoided experiencing in my last life, I ended up experiencing in this one. But now, the rabbi continued, my suffering, like the Holocaust itself, was over. Whatever lessons the Almighty had intended for me to learn through suffering have already been learned.

I felt tremendously released by this insight. And indeed, since our conversation, my life has moved on. The harsh experiences of my life no longer color my days with sadness and pain. Instead, they have been transformed through the years into resources of insight, tolerance, and understanding—with a little wisdom here and there.

It has not been easy to openly discuss my dream and its interpretation with those who matter most to me. In fact, it has taken me a long time to overcome my personal bias against this “foreign” idea. Talking about reincarnation in this day and age puts me right in the middle of the fringe. After all, who, in the Western world, believes in that stuff? My response—and the response of every American Jew I ever knew—used to be, “Crackpots and new-agers maybe, but not Jews.” Most people have been as surprised as I was to discover that Jews can believe in reincarnation.

During part of my adult life, I had come to revere cold science more than G-d. But I eventually arrived at a point where I had to consider how quantum theory is bringing us ever closer to a new way of looking at time and matter. Einstein revealed the theory of relativity, mathematically proving that time is more flexible than we think it is. Heisenberg proposed the uncertainty principle, demonstrating that matter doesn’t always behave in ways we can measure. As a consequence of these and other scientific discoveries, the apparent gap between knowledge and faith is narrowing. It no longer takes such a great leap of imagination to accept the possibility that souls might step in and out of time, in accordance with a greater spiritual law. For me, accepting the mystical structure of the universe is merely acknowledging the power of an unknowable G-d. I find great comfort and endless peace in that.

Chapter 14:

Keepers of the Joy

by Patricia (Rachel Brachah) O'Brian

I do not have clear, specific memories of a past life in the Holocaust. However, I do remember reading books about the Holocaust as a child. When I saw the pictures of the concentration camp victims, I was both compelled and repelled. The scenes would be vaguely familiar to me, but I could not recall having been in a specific camp or time period. Yet I would sometimes be seized by intense feelings of hunger, cold, and fear. I have also been terrified whenever I have had to cross dark, open fields. I feel as if something is pursuing me . . .

What I do recall from childhood is having a strong attraction to Judaism, which goes as far back as I can remember. I came from a relatively anti-Semitic family and went to Catholic school, where I prayed to be delivered from "the perfidious Jew and the infidel." I was also taught that only Catholics go to heaven.

On the day that I learned that particular dogma, I went to the church after school and had a long mental argument with G-d.[1] I remember telling Him that although

He was All-Powerful and All-Knowing, He was still pretty mean and stupid. How could He punish people for not being Catholic, when He had made us all the way we were in the first place? Such deep musings from a seven-year-old theologian were not well received by the nuns, but I was very good at recognizing inconsistencies.

In third grade, I was finally introduced to "Bible history." This was a welcome change from two previous years of rote recitation of the *Baltimore Catechism.* Now we learned the stories of the patriarchs (Abraham, Isaac, and Jacob) and matriarchs (Sarah, Rebecca, Rachel, and Leah). How I thrilled to those stories: Joseph and Pharoah, Joshua at Jericho, the binding of Isaac, and the Exodus from Egypt—they seemed so real to me.

I felt a deep connection to the people of ancient Israel and couldn't learn enough about them. So I went to the public library every day after school and read every book I could find about Jewish history, religion, customs, and holidays. The more I read, the more the joy spread through every cell of my young body. In Catholic school, I had never agreed with what the nuns taught me about G-d and religion. So I had developed my own ideas and thought I was alone in them. Now I learned that what I believed was the same as what Judaism taught. I wasn't alone. I wasn't crazy—I was Jewish!

* * *

Over the years, I continued to study, and in adulthood I finally took the important step of formal conversion to Judaism. "Conversion"—how I despise that term! I prefer to call it "homecoming." I have developed my own *midrash* [parable] about this homecoming, to explain why some people are born directly into the Jewish tribe, while others must come to it through "conversion."

In the 29th chapter of Deuteronomy, Moses said to the people:

> *Atem nitzavim hayom chulchem*—today *all of you* are standing before YHVH your G-d: your heads, your tribes, your elders, and your officers—all the men of Israel, and your little ones, your wives, *and the stranger that is in the midst of your camp,* from the hewer of wood to the drawer of water—to enter into the Covenant of YHVH your G-d . . . that He may establish you as a people unto Him, and He may be a G-d to you.[2]

The classical *Midrash* (Rabbinic commentary) seeks to further expand and explain these verses of the Torah. According to one well-known interpretation, "all of you" means that the soul of every Jew who ever was (or would be) born was present at Mt. Sinai, when G-d revealed the Torah, and the Jewish people accepted His Covenant. The reference to "the stranger" refers to Gentiles who also accepted the Torah and would later find their way to Judaism.[3]

My personal *midrash* takes this idea one step further. I believe that Ha-Shem [a name for G-d] foresaw the trials and tribulations that would befall the Jewish people. He also knew that there would be many who would come to see Judaism as a horrible burden, as something to be cast off at the earliest opportunity. So G-d called aside some of the Jewish souls at Mt. Sinai and asked if they would be willing to accept temporary separation from their own people and be born into the non-Jewish world. These souls would retain their intuitive knowledge and memory of the joys of Judaism and would be increasingly drawn toward it, to eventually rejoin the tribe in a later incarnation. Yet their path would be very difficult, for they would have to endure a long and painful exile.

I call these souls the *Shomrei Simchah*—"Keepers of the Joy." Throughout the ages, these "Keepers" would live as Jewish souls in Gentile bodies, until the moment came for them to act as a "time-release" medicine for their people. Whenever the spirit of the Jews became hopelessly crushed under the yoke of persecution and oppression, then some of these "time-release Jews" would find their way back to Judaism and "convert." Because their spirits were not burdened by centuries of persecution, they would also bring a fresh new perspective, to help revitalize Judaism with their joy.

I see myself as one of these "Keepers," who has returned to my people in a time when the joy is eclipsed by the painful memory of the Holocaust. My path has not been easy. Some of my "born Jewish" friends are amazed and slightly annoyed at what they consider to be my "overzealous commitment." Others have called me crazy and worse, incredulous that anyone would willingly choose to be a Jew. At times, the collective pain of the Holocaust seems to hang over the Jewish community like a dark, ominous cloud.[4]

Once, a rabbi asked me why I wanted to take on the "burdens" and "restrictions" of the Torah.[5] Now it was my turn to be incredulous, because I find the Torah to be the most liberating force in my life. When I hold a Torah scroll in my arms and dance with it on Simchat Torah, or sit in the fragile shelter of the *sukkah* booth, or put on my *tallis* and *tefillin*[6] to pray, I cry tears of joy because of the abundance of spiritual riches which Judaism gives to me.

As I light the candles every Friday night, I am filled with awe to realize that I stand together with Jewish women all over the world—and throughout all time—who also performed this simple ritual to usher in the Sabbath. All of these ceremonies are indescribably beautiful to me, perhaps because I can remember them from the days of Sinai, before they were "spoiled" by the shaming scorn of anti-Semites.

* * *

In order to complete my conversion process, I had to appear before a *bet din* (rabbinical court) and go to the mikveh, a type of ritual immersion. According to Jewish law, at the moment I emerged from the mikveh's "living waters," I had become a Jew.

In the legal sense that is true. But in my heart I have always been a Jew—ever since the Torah was given at Mt. Sinai. My journey through the centuries has been long and tiring, and I arrived so dusty and disheveled that nobody was able to recognize me. No, the mikveh did not "make" me a Jew—it just washed the dirt away, so that everyone could see my true identity.

I now believe that G-d had planned it this way, so many millennia ago. My soul shivers at pictures of the Holocaust, because it has been spiritually connected to the Jews for all these many centuries. Now the time has come, at last, for me to return and serve my people, by helping them to move beyond the trauma and rediscover the joys of Jewishness. I know the task will not be easy. Still, it's great to be home at last!

Chapter 15:

The Circle of Torah

by Yonassan Gershom

This book would not be complete without my own story about letting go. For the past fifteen years, the subject of Holocaust reincarnation has dominated my consciousness to the point that I sometimes neglected other important areas in my life. As I explained in the introduction to this book, I did not set out to become the "Holocaust reincarnation rabbi." In the beginning, I was simply a Hasidic storyteller who was willing to listen to some very strange tales. And, as every shaman knows, through "the telling of the vision" in the right time and place, the wounded spirit can be healed. I was always a willing participant in this process but, as the years passed, I became so typecast in the role that I despaired of ever moving beyond it. Now the time has come for me to do so.

My personal journey from ashes to healing has been long and difficult. It was not easy for me to hear about so many nightmares, visions, and vivid past-life memories of torture and betrayal. Many have been the nights that I went to bed extremely depressed, asking my Creator why I had been given this overwhelmingly sad burden. On one such night, I had the following dream, which I first reported in *Beyond the Ashes:*

> I dreamed that I was a young Hasidic boy, about eight or nine years old, living in Eastern Europe. The Jews of the village had gathered together, and we could hear the sounds of battle in the distance. My father, who was the village rabbi, was trying to comfort the people. He explained that although they were about to die, they should not be afraid, because the body is only a garment. The soul, he said, lives forever and will one day return to earth in a new garment.
>
> But the rabbi explained sadly that there was a problem. For many, many incarnations, their souls had returned to this same village to be reborn as their children's children. This time, however, the village would be destroyed completely, and none would survive to provide new bodies for the souls. They could never come back to this place and might, therefore, become separated from one another in the next life. How would they ever find each other again?
>
> It was decided to draw straws. The person thus chosen would incarnate immediately and look for a new place for the villagers to return to. After preparing the way, he would serve as a psychic beacon for the other souls, who would seek him out. In this way, it was hoped, the villagers would not become lost to one another.
>
> Solemnly the Jews said a prayer together, then each took a straw, while the sounds of battle drew closer and closer. Suddenly everyone gasped—I

> had drawn the short straw! Just as I was about to protest that I was too young and didn't know how, the Nazis entered the village and began shooting everyone. Then I woke up.[1]

Over the years, I have deeply contemplated this dream, which eventually became the paradigm for understanding my role in the Holocaust reincarnation story. If, as I now believe, my dream was really a past-life memory, then I was far more than a "rabbi's son." My father in that life was the Rebbe—spiritual master—of the village, and I would have inherited the position from him. Had I survived the Holocaust, I would now be an elderly man in my mid-70s. And in so many ways, that's exactly what I am, even though the body I now wear was born in 1947. Throughout my life, I have always related best to people who were decades older than I. Like so many of the people in this book, I, too, was a stranger to my family of birth, and I remain a loner to this day.

A Muslim Sufi teacher once told me that we spend the first half of our lives cleaning up karma from the last incarnation and the next half preparing for our future life. In my own case, I know this to be true. For almost five decades I have tried, in one way or another, to re-create the little village of my soul memories. Many years ago, when I first met Rabbi Zalman Schachter, I thought that I had found it at last. There was such an overpowering feeling of "instant recognition" in those first moments together! In spite of the fact that Reb Zalman is twenty years my senior, I have always felt that we are of the same generation.

Reb Zalman recognized our soul affinity, too. For two decades I was his devoted disciple. In 1983, he empowered me as a spiritual director, and in 1986 I was personally ordained by him in the B'nai Or ("Children of Light") movement that he had founded. But not long after that joyous occasion, the original B'nai Or ceased to be neo-Hasidic and became, instead, the "Aleph Alliance for Jewish Renewal," a non-Orthodox network that my heart could not embrace. Reb Zalman sensed my distress and gave me a double blessing to go my own way. We parted as friends and have remained so, but I was spiritually homeless again.

Next followed a number of unsuccessful attempts to found an alternative Jewish community—experiments which are best left to sleep in the dust of forgotten history. When *Beyond the Ashes* was finally published in 1992, many people who read my dream about the village interpreted it as a sign for me to found a more universal "new age" community. Had I wanted to start my own cult, it would have been easy. But I knew in my heart that this wasn't the will of God for me. I did not come back to found a "new-age" sect.

I have always felt that my dream is about *Jewish continuity,* not breaking with tradition. My work with Holocaust past-life issues has led me ever deeper into Hasidism and has strengthened my commitment to the Torah way of life. If those villagers from another life do meet with me again, it will not be as cultists in some esoteric movement, but as the religious Jews that they have been for generations of incarnations. For them, as for me, the bond formed at Sinai is an everlasting covenant that must not be broken.

The other part of the dream—the part which usually gets overlooked by the interpreters—is that I came back *one generation early.* My role was not to re-create the village now, but to prepare the way for it to happen in the future. My vow was to become a bridge between what was lost in the Holocaust and what exists now in America. In that, I have more than succeeded. But a strong bridge must be firmly anchored on both sides of the river and, by doing so, it can belong to neither. As a Lakota medicine man once told me, "The shaman always walks alone."

When the villagers and I drew straws on that day in another life, we really did believe that we could meet somewhere in the future and pick up where we left off. What we failed to foresee was how devastated our people would be when they emerged from the dark tunnel that was the Nazi Holocaust. I now understand that it will take us many incarnations to become whole once again.

If "my" villagers are on earth at all, then they are not in my own generation. Perhaps they are just now being born. In recent years I have met many Jewish children with that far-off "knowing" look in their eyes—old souls in young bodies, who resonate deeply with the language, ceremonies, and practices of the traditional way of life. In the postwar days of my childhood, Jewishness was an embarrassment. But to this new generation, it is a source of pride. As a community, we are finally beginning to heal.

My personal closure came on the festival of Simchat Torah—"Rejoicing in the Teachings"—in the fall of 1995. During this annual celebration, we take out the Torah scrolls and dance with them in joyous processions. Believe me, those parchment scrolls are heavy—some weigh forty pounds or more—but when a Jew dances with joy, then "the Torah carries itself." On the physical level, of course, people take turns carrying the scrolls, while others dance around them in circles, chanting sacred verses over and over in Hebrew, like a mantra.

On this particular weekend, I was speaking at a conference in Baltimore, Maryland. Jewish law forbids traveling on the major holy days and, because Simchat Torah would begin on Sunday evening that year, there was no time to fly back to Minnesota. Laurie Schwartz, the conference coordinator, had graciously arranged for me to spend the holiday in the Orthodox section of Baltimore, at a little Hasidic synagogue led by Rabbi Menachem Goldberger.

In some congregations, the Simchat Torah festivities border on revelry, but at the Goldberger shul, the mantra songs and "mitzvah dances" were taken very seriously. The Rebbe personally began each song alone, closing his eyes and setting the tempo with completely focused attention. Then the congregation joined in, first singing and then dancing the same tune together for half an hour or more. In accordance with Orthodox practice, there were no musical instruments, only the sounds of singing voices, clapping hands, and hundreds of stomping feet. As individual dancers became tired, they would drop out of the circle and were immediately replaced by others, but the dance itself went on into the night.

To dance in such a circle can be a transcendental experience. It certainly was for me. As my feet were caught up in the rhythm at the Goldberger shul, my mind went back to another Simchat Torah, several years before, at the University of Minnesota Hillel House. There they have a "Holocaust Torah," a two-hundred-year-old scroll that was confiscated by the Nazis, then rescued and given a place of honor in the Hillel chapel. The one and only time I ever held that scroll was also on Simchat Torah. As I cradled it in my arms like a child, I could literally feel the souls of all the Jews who had ever carried it when it was still in Eastern Europe. I felt my spirit join with theirs, as my soul soared with such complete ecstasy that words could never describe it.

Dancing around me at the Hillel celebration was a circle of college students, completely unaware of my "psychic experience" with the scroll. Suddenly I felt an overwhelming urge to carry the Holocaust Torah outside and dance with it under the stars, like they used to do in Russia and still do in New York and Israel. The Hillel building has a stone patio in front, so I signaled to others in the circle, and, forming a joyful procession, we headed for the door. Soon we were dancing *horas* right there on "fraternity row," where the usual noise is from beer parties, not sacred singing.

Once again, I felt the presence of Jewish souls on the "other side," now filled with great rejoicing, as if this were a spiritual healing, both for the Torah scroll and for the souls of those who had honored it on earth. Later that evening I was told that this was the first time Jews on that campus had ever proudly danced in front of the building like that. Now it happens every year.

My mind returned to the present celebration in Baltimore, where my body was dancing with a Hasidic rabbi whose spiritual heritage traces back to the Rebbe of Chernobyl.[2] In Chernobyl today, there are no more Hasidim. But the dance which began there still goes on, across the ocean and around the globe. To the Gentile world, "Chernobyl" is now a symbol of nuclear disaster. But in the Hasidic world, Chernobyl remains a place where the spiritual light once shone brightly and still lives in the hearts of the people. From circle to circle and from life to life, the Torah is passed down, and the sacred dance continues.

When I came home from Baltimore, I knew what I must do. It was time for me to retire from reincarnation counseling, so that I could rejoin the dance and move from ashes to healing. For fifteen years, I have been somewhat outside the Hasidic circle, bridging the old and the new. In doing that, I became a magnet for wounded souls who found their way to my doorstep. But nowadays, it is the secular therapists, not the Hasidic

Rebbes, who make careers of past-life counseling and healing. My mission accomplished, I now pass the torch that I have carried for fifteen years.

By writing these books and "breaking the ice" on a subject that was taboo in therapeutic circles, I gave others permission to come out of the closet with their stories about mystical encounters with the Holocaust. In so doing, I fulfilled my vow to become a "psychic beacon" in this transitional generation. Through this sharing, there has been wonderful healing and closure for all of us. Whether we "tell the vision" around the campfire, at the Sabbath table, or in the therapy circle, it is through the process itself that the healing happens. I was never more than a willing catalyst, who created a safe place for God—the True Divine Physician and Source of All Healing—to work His miracles. In the end, I remain what I have always been: a simple storyteller.

> "Thou has turned my mourning into dancing;
> Thou has put off my sackcloth,
> and girded me with gladness." (Psalm 30:11)

Appendix A:

The Jewish Soul

by Rabbi Yonassan Gershom

According to classical Judaism, when God gave the Torah to the Jews at Mt. Sinai, this was a cosmic event that changed the nature of the universe forever. All the souls of all the Jews who ever were or would be born were present at Sinai, either in the flesh or in the spirit. As one people, they accepted the Covenant with God, not only for themselves but for all future generations to come. In the words of Moses in the Book of Deuteronomy: "It was not only with our ancestors that God (YHVH) made this Covenant, but with us, the living, every one of us here today."[1]

The Jewish mystics (both kabbalists and Hasidim) took this idea even further. By reading "generations" as a veiled reference to "incarnations," they broadened the Covenant at Sinai to include not only one's genetic descendants, but also one's future lives. In that way, the "merits of our ancestors" became our own merits, and the "sins of the ancestors" became our own karma from a previous life.

Central to this kabbalistic understanding of the Bible is the idea that the souls who were "standing at Sinai" became—and will remain—Jewish for all incarnations. Seen from this perspective, rebirth into a non-Jewish body represents a very serious form of exile, a state of being literally "cut off" *(karet)* from one's own people. On the other hand, a Gentile who converts to Judaism is seen as a lost soul on its way back home.[2]

Many of the Holocaust reincarnation stories seem to bear this out. In her essay for this book, "Keepers of the Joy," Patricia O'Brian described how her conversion to Judaism was really more like a homecoming. O'Brian, like so many other converts who have shared their stories with me, firmly believes that her soul has always been Jewish since Sinai, no matter what type of body it wore. Over the past fifteen years, hundreds of other people have expressed similar feelings to me about being "Jewish souls in Gentile bodies."

A high percentage of these same people also feel completely alienated from their families and cultures of birth. I would even go so far as to say that this feeling of alienation is *the* most driving force which compels such seekers to contact me as a rabbi. In so many cases, secular therapy simply is not enough. Nevertheless, because the idea of a "Jewish soul" flies in the face of current "new age" theology, many people on the speaking circuit have taken me to task for teaching it. In all fairness, I must point out that belief in an "ethnic soul" is not limited to Jews alone.

For example, the Druses, who have always kept their religion secret until very recently, firmly believe that "a Druse will always be reborn a Druse." Because the Druses also expect to be reborn immediately after death, their children often remember vivid, accurate details about the life just prior to this one. Sometimes these children are also recognized by still-living relatives from their last life. So common is this phenomenon that Druse law specifically excludes inheritance claims based upon relationships from previous incarnations![3]

In addition to the Druses, many other tribal cultures, including both Native American and African peoples, also believe in an "ethnic soul." The late James "Jimmie" Jackson, a well-respected Ojibwa medicine man from Minnesota, taught that American Indian souls can and should retain their tribal identity after death. In his work with Ojibwa youth, he frequently stressed the importance of having an Indian name, in order to find one's relatives in the next world. At the moment of death, Jimmie explained, everyone follows a road with two sets of tracks, one made by moccasins and the other by shoes. At the place where these two trails fork, a spirit being speaks Ojibwa to the soul and asks for its Indian name. If the soul cannot understand the language or remember the name, then it must follow the shoe tracks and go with the white people instead.[4]

This story is exactly like the teaching about Dumah, the "Angel of the Grave," who meets the souls of the Jewish dead and asks for their Hebrew names. Souls who forget their Hebrew names must then "wander among the Gentiles" until they remember who they really are. For this reason, many traditional Jews memorize biblical acrostics which spell out their Hebrew names. The reasoning behind this practice is that the words of the Torah are eternal, so the acrostic will not fade from memory after death. Also at the moment of death, it is customary to whisper the Hebrew name into the ear of the deceased. The sense of hearing, as science now confirms, is the last to go in the dying process.

* * *

In contrast to this tribal perspective, Western metaphysics currently teaches that the soul has no permanent cultural identity, but is supposed to shed its ethnicity with the death of the body. The soul then goes "into the light," where it rests in a generic interlife, until it voluntarily chooses to return to earth in a new body. According to this model, the karmic bond among souls is not membership in a religion or tribe, but rather, the interpersonal relationships among the souls themselves.

This theory has great appeal to students of metaphysics in the United States, where the majority of citizens come from a mixed heritage and are not strongly connected to any particular tribe or culture. In addition, many "new agers" now see the tribal belief in an "ethnic soul" as backward and narrow-minded. However, with the recent rise in multicultural awareness, I believe we must now reexamine many basic assumptions about "universal" spirituality.

From the standpoint of anthropology, Abbye Silverstein's story about Jewish souls living in spirit villages ("The Healer Heals Herself") reflects themes which are very similar to the well-known visions of Wovoka, the nineteenth-century Paiute Indian holy man who founded the Ghost Dance religion. In Wovoka's version of the "World to Come," the white man was gone forever, the buffalo had returned, and the Indians were free to follow the Good Red Road of peace and plenty—*without the interference of the European conquerors.* Far from depicting a "universal" heaven where everyone was the same, Wovoka's paradise was a return to the old ways of his people.

Similarly, in Silverstein's scenario, the anti-Semites were completely gone, the burned-out villages were rebuilt, and the Jews were free to follow the Way of the Torah in peace. Like the visions of Wovoka, Silverstein's interlife experience also affirmed the survival of her people's identity. Both of these "Heavens" express the hopes of an oppressed people for self-determination, along with a belief that the collective identity of the tribe and its members will endure beyond the grave.

Concerning reincarnation, many North American Indians not only want to come back into the same tribe, they expect to be reborn within the same family lines. According to parapsychologist Antonia Mills of the University of Virginia, this belief is so common among Native Americans that it poses a serious problem for scientists who want to study Indian children with past-life memories. "It's very difficult in general," Mills said, "to be sure that the statement a child makes [about a past life] is not based on knowledge the child could learn from its parents or other relatives."[5]

Like the Native Americans, many traditional Jews also expect to come back in their own family lines, which is one reason that the position of Hasidic Rebbe is usually passed from father to son. Rabbi Nachman of Breslov, the great-grandson of the Baal Shem Tov, was believed by some to be the reincarnation of that very same soul. Reb Nachman himself never made this claim, but always insisted that his greatness was due to his own efforts.[6] Still, the fact that he was a child prodigy leaves us wondering: Were "his own efforts" limited to this life alone?

Be that as it may, both Jewish and Native American souls seem to prefer returning in the same genetic lines. And therein lies an interesting question. What happens when entire family trees—even whole tribes—are completely wiped off the face of the planet, so that no visible trace of their gene pool remains?

I have heard Native American shamans tell stories about "Indian souls" who were separated from their own people when smallpox epidemics wiped out the entire tribe. With no trace of the tribal gene pool left, these souls went elsewhere to reincarnate, *but retained their Indian identities.* During the 1960s, this was a common explanation for the sudden interest in native cultures by white middle-class hippies. On more than one occasion, I was told by native shamans that these "white Indians" were the souls of warriors who had died in the previous century.

Interestingly, a high percentage of these "white Indians" also claim to have a genetic ancestor who married an Indian—a common occurrence on the American frontier. Similarly, in cases where Jews have come back as Gentiles, they often discover a "forgotten" Jewish ancestor on the family tree.

According to a fourteenth-century kabbalistic text, the *Sefer Ha'pliya* ("Book of Marvels"), a Jewish soul which is somehow "cut off" from its people does sometimes return as its own great-grandchild. When we consider the enormous rate of intermarriage in America and the tendency for immigrants to drop their ethnic identities, then the chances are very good that many non-Jews have a "lost" Jewish ancestor. Rabbi Allen Maller has documented a number of such cases in his excellent book, *God, Sex, and Kabbalah.*[7] It could also be that some Holocaust victims were so desperate to remain connected to their people, no matter how tenuously, that they sought out any lineage they could find with even a single Jew in it.

From an empirical standpoint—provided we accept the evidence of past-life regression—numerous examples can be found to support both the "ethnic soul" and the "universalist" theories. On the one hand, the same soul has apparently served as the Dalai Lama, head of Tibetan Buddhism, for fourteen incarnations. That soul, in turn, is accompanied by a cluster of other souls, who serve him as Tibetan monks.[8] On the other hand, Westerners frequently claim a long list of lives in a smorgasbord of cultures. Apparently some souls travel from tribe to tribe for a "general education," while others remain in one tradition to become specialized.

In addition, because "like attracts like" on the spiritual path, there is probably a strong tendency for souls with similar agendas to seek each other out from one lifetime to the next. When Rabbi Israel Baal Shem Tov, the founder of Hasidism, "saw" the past lives of his closest disciples, those lives were always Jewish. I believe this was because, like the monks who serve the Dalai Lama, the souls who surrounded the Baal Shem Tov had been working together as Jews for many incarnations. The very nature of the Baal Shem Tov's work required a circle of devoted Hasidim who could learn and understand Torah on the deepest, most intuitive levels. It's a rare soul in any religious discipline that can develop such expertise in a single lifetime.

In contrast, the Edgar Cayce readings contain many stories of clients who had wandered from culture to culture in their previous lives. I find myself asking: Was there something about Cayce himself which attracted such souls to him? Or was it simply because America is a land where eclecticism is highly encouraged?

In Edgar Cayce's day, the "melting pot" model of America was still in vogue, and "multiculturalism," as we know it today, simply did not exist. Immigrants were expected to Americanize their names, give up their native languages, and throw their ethnic identities overboard as they entered New York Harbor. This attitude of "Americanization," combined with the widespread Christian belief that "in Christ there is neither Jew nor Greek," probably attracted souls who saw such assimilation as the golden path to freedom. In turn, the preponderance of these types of cases in the Cayce readings has caused many people to assume that they are representative of all populations and cultures.

Nowadays, however, serious problems can arise when the two worldviews—cultural diversity and assimilation—collide on the spiritual path. Secular past-life therapists frequently tell me that, if a Jewish soul opts for a life as a non-Jew, then this is a "positive learning experience" that will bring about a "more universal" perspective. In some cases that may well be true. But to define all souls as "limited" if they choose to specialize in one path is utterly ludicrous. By that definition, the Dalai Lama would be among the most "narrow" and "limited" of all, since he has spent his previous thirteen lives—if not all of his other incarnations, too—in the isolated mountains of Tibet! Clearly, a spiritual smorgasbord is not necessary to become an enlightened being.

* * *

How, then, can we better understand the need for some souls to remain Jewish from one life to the next? As we previously learned, the souls of the Jews were all present—in body or in spirit—when the Torah was given at Mt. Sinai. Also, according to Jewish teachings, those souls from Sinai are like the letters in a Torah scroll. On the one hand, each "letter" is uniquely handwritten by God, with its own individuality and special place in the story. At the same time, the letters join with each other to form a greater whole. If even one "letter" is missing, then the entire scroll is considered "defective" and cannot be used until it has been "repaired" and "made whole" once again.

For this reason, the Christian idea that "I am saved but you will go to Hell" is completely alien to Jewish thought.

"All Jews are responsible for one another," the well-known saying goes. The Jews, in turn, are responsible for *tikkun olam*—"repairing the world." Once enlightened, the true Hasidic master, like the Buddhist *boddhisatva,* is expected to forego Heaven for himself until everyone "written in the scroll" is also ready to go.

When Rabbi Moshe Teitelbaum, the first Satmar Rebbe, was lying on his deathbed, he found himself thinking about the holy teachers who had gone before him to Paradise. "Why do they keep silence up there?" the Rebbe asked. "Why don't they shake all the upper worlds and bring the Messiah down to earth?"

The Rebbe sighed and closed his eyes. He was very, very close to death now, perhaps even glimpsing his own place in the World to Come . . . Suddenly he opened his eyes wide and exclaimed, "In the realm of delight they have been so deluged with joy that they have completely forgotten the earth. But even if they try to do the same to me—I shall not abandon my people!"[9]

Even more poignant is the deathbed story of Rabbi Nachman of Breslov, whose last words on earth were, "I am not leaving you, Heaven forbid!" According to his disciples, he has kept his word. Although Nachman's body died, his soul remains "between the worlds," voluntarily forsaking the rewards of Paradise in order to guide and comfort his disciples on earth. To this very day, Nachman is still "the Rebbe" to Breslover Hasidim, and many wonderful stories are told about personal encounters with his spirit.[10]

Of course, not everyone has the fortitude to be a Rebbe Nachman. If even the great Hasidic masters can "forget the earth" in the bliss of Paradise, then perhaps we cannot fault those lesser souls who "abandoned their people" under the hellish duress of the Holocaust. But at the same time, I cannot help but be saddened whenever

I hear how a soul was so deeply wounded by the Nazis that it chose not be Jewish anymore. Such a decision might well be a "learning experience," but it is also a deep tragedy.

* * *

In addition to the question about whether or not Jews can return as non-Jews or vice versa, there is a more ominous pattern of thought about the Holocaust, now emerging in some esoteric circles. My correspondence files are filled with "channeled" claims that Nazis have supposedly returned as Israeli soldiers, as starving Ethiopians, as victims of "ethnic cleansing" in Bosnia, as perpetrators of the same . . . Somehow, there is a great deal of inconsistency in all of this "channeling." How can the Nazis be returning as both the oppressors and their victims at the same time?

When dealing with "channeled" material, we must always ask ourselves: Is this information *really* based on karmic truth from the Mind of God, or is it merely a projection of our own subconscious beliefs and stereotypes? It may well be that starving Ethiopians *look like* the "living skeletons" from concentration camps, but that does not necessarily mean that every victim of famine has a karmic connection with the Holocaust! I believe it is very important to make a distinction between genuine past-life memories and archetypal symbolism from the collective unconscious.

An even more disturbing theory, now circulating in some esoteric circles, is the idea that Jews who died in the concentration camps are returning as neo-Nazis to seek revenge. Granted, this might happen in a few isolated cases. But the majority of Jews were so deeply traumatized under the swastika, that it seems unlikely they would be attracted to this symbol in their present lives. For Lena-Marie Broman ("Flashbacks in Vienna") and many others like her, the very thought of Nazi flags triggered intense fear and disgust.

Secular research on reincarnation, such as that of Dr. Ian Stevenson at the University of Virginia, seems to suggest that we are not drawn to the "opposite" of what we once were, but to *that which is familiar from the previous life.* Dr. Stevenson describes cases of Burmese children who remember being Japanese soldiers during World War II and who still crave Japanese food. "The Burmese have weak tea," Stevenson explains, "but the Japanese characteristically want strong tea and a lot of sugar in it. These children will ask for this strong tea and for raw fish [a Japanese favorite] and they grumble about the spice in the Burmese food."[11]

Past-life therapist Barbara Lane has found similar patterns in her work with American Civil War reenactors. In her new book, *Echoes from the Battlefield* (A.R.E. Press, 1996), she analyzes twelve cases of individuals who had an incarnation in the Civil War period (1860s) and are still attracted to the history, clothing, and lifestyles of that era. All of her clients regularly participate in "living history" reenactment battles and other events, and they repeatedly stated that they felt more comfortable wearing Civil War clothing. Most had spent a great deal of time and money to duplicate uniforms and other garb, as well as the paraphernalia necessary to reenact the battles. For these people, "living history" events are much more than theatre. They are opportunities to step back into the lost world of a previous life.

In a similar way, I believe that some souls who were Nazis in World War II are still attracted to fascism, perhaps resonating with the swastika as a familiar symbol from their "glory days" in the Third Reich. If such souls are seeking revenge, it is not for being abused as Jews in the concentration camps, but for the "humiliation" of losing the war to the Allies.[12]

As the firsthand stories in this book clearly demonstrate, karma is not always tit for tat, nor do we necessarily flip back and forth between victim and oppressor roles. In Linda Thieman's story ("To Triumph over Evil"), the same two souls lived the same two roles of "master and slave" for three incarnations—from the Roman Empire to Nazi Germany to a marriage made in Kuwait. Healing finally came when Linda was able to let go of this abusive relationship. And, please note, she was aided by Jewish spirits who came to her, not for revenge, but to help send Holocaust souls into the light!

In conclusion, I feel we must be very careful not to project "white middle-class values" onto our understanding of reincarnation. Belief in rebirth has only recently returned to the Western world, while among many tribal and village societies—including Hasidic Jews—it was never lost. It may well be that these traditional cultures have preserved levels of understanding about the cycles of rebirth that have been lost to Western metaphysics. Rather than dismiss one interpretation or the other as "wrong," we should view them all as essential parts of a richly woven tapestry. In the words of the Talmud, "*Eleh v'eleh divrei elokim chai*—both this and this are the words of the living God."

Appendix B:

Did the Soul of Hitler Repent?

by Rabbi Yonassan Gershom

When I was growing up in the 1950s, Adolf Hitler was the ultimate personification of evil. Like Haman in the Purim story, Hitler was the archetypal villain; if I had believed in the devil, then he would have looked exactly like Hitler.

The point at which I began to see Hitler as a human being came much later, when I read Alice Miller's classic treatise on child abuse, *For Your Own Good.* In that book, Miller explored Hitler's early childhood and came to the conclusion that abuse by his father, Alois Hitler, had set little Adolf on a course of self-destruction that led to the abuse of millions when he became the Führer of Nazi Germany. The German people followed him, according to Miller, because they had been conditioned by Victorian child-rearing techniques to submit unquestioningly to authority.

Reading Miller's analysis of Hitler's childhood did not lessen the horrors of the Holocaust for me, but it did arouse my curiosity about the human side of the man.

My personal grapplings with the psychology of Hitler resulted in the following dream, which came in the fall of 1989, just before Yom Kippur, and was eventually published in *Beyond the Ashes:*

> In 1989 I had a very vivid dream, in which I was standing in the lobby of a theater. I was dressed in the Sabbath garb of a Hasidic Rebbe, complete with long black coat, fur hat, and side curls. The name of the play I had come to see was "The Life and Times of Adolf Hitler." All of the people in the audience had already gone inside, and I was alone.
>
> Just as the house lights were dimmed and the play was about to begin, Hitler himself walked in off the street. I expected to be frightened, but somehow I was not. Hitler looked very small, tired, and sad, as if he no longer had any will to live. He picked up a copy of the theater program and walked over to me.
>
> "Look what they are saying about me!" Hitler lamented, pointing to the list of acts from the play about his life. I looked at the piece of paper and saw that all the things Hitler had done were listed there, in chronological order, scene by scene.
>
> "Yes," I replied. "That is how you are remembered on earth." A terrible look of pain came over Hitler's face. Then he broke down and began to sob like a heartbroken child. At first I thought to myself, "It serves him right," but then, before I even knew what I was doing, I had put my arms around the sobbing Hitler and was comforting him. I explained that if he were truly repentant, then the door to forgiveness was open to him the same as any other sinner, but the road would be very, very difficult. Hitler nodded in agreement, expressing his willingness to try.

> At that moment, a van arrived outside the theater, and a dark-skinned man, a retarded boy, and an old woman in a wheelchair came out and entered the lobby. They said, "We have come to take him to the next level." Hitler left with the three people, and they all drove away in the van. Then I woke up.[1]

At the time, I interpreted the dream as an allegory about my own struggles with forgiving the Nazis—nothing more. In fact, the dream wasn't even included in the first draft of *Beyond the Ashes* because I didn't think it was important to anyone but myself. It had been triggered, I assumed, by the intense focus on repentance during the High Holy Day season. Only much later, after my editor suggested that I expand on the theme of "What happened to Nazi souls?" did I decide to include my personal dream about forgiving Hitler.

Then in 1994—two years after *Beyond the Ashes* finally came out—I received a very strange phone call from a psychic named Michael Schuster, who claimed to be "channeling" the repentant soul of Hitler. To be perfectly honest, I thought he was a crackpot. Who wouldn't? Nevertheless, I remained on the line and listened to his story. The more he told me about these "Hitler channelings," the more I began to wonder if there might not be something to it.

There was a karmic connection, Schuster claimed, between the timing of my dream and the "awakening" of the soul of Hitler from decades of self-imposed isolation in the spirit world. Hitler's "awakening" had also occurred in the fall of 1989, *at a time when I had not yet told anyone about my dream!* As Schuster later wrote:

> I do not consider Rabbi Gershom's encounter just

> a dream! From what I know of Hitler's frame of mind in 1989 and the nature of the between-life environment, the Rabbi's "astral journey" reveals Hitler's attempted healing after emerging from his self-created bunker.
>
> In his first contact with earth since his death, Hitler sought out a rabbi who could find compassion in his heart.[2]

Perhaps it was my ego speaking, but I was intrigued. Was it really possible that my inner struggles were somehow connected to the repentance of Hitler's soul? To even think such a thing seemed like megalomania! And yet, this was the very stuff of which Hasidic stories are made . . . Besides, didn't my own religion teach that even Amalek—the very epitome of evil—could repent if he chose to do so? *How would I react, I asked myself, if that really happened?* In the end, my curiosities won out, and I agreed to accept a copy of Schuster's new book, *Conversations with Adolf Hitler.*

By the time the book arrived, my skepticism had returned in full force, and Schuster's autobiography in the preface did little to reassure me. Like so many "new age" mystics, he claims to be a "walk-in," a discarnate spirit who took over "Old Michael's" physical body after he "died" on the operating table after a car accident in 1964. "Old Michael" was a Jewish teenager, who was called "kike" and worse during his childhood in America. "New Michael"—the "walk-in"—claims to be the soul of Thomas Goettenberg, a Nazi SS officer convicted of war crimes, who died in a Russian prison in 1947. The current "Michael Schuster," according to his own account, is a blend of these two entities—the Jew and the Nazi—and their past-life memories from World War II.

I freely admit that I do not believe in "walk-ins" as

such. At best, the idea strikes me as a form of fantasy or disassociation, perhaps even a multiple personality disorder. At worst, the "walk-in" could actually be a *dybbuk,* an evil entity which possesses the body of a living person to fulfill its own selfish ends. I have participated in exorcisms, and I believe in *dybbuks.* I also believe that the spirit of a holy sage—in Jewish terms, an *ibbur*—might work through an individual on a temporary basis, for the purpose of accomplishing a specific task. But an *ibbur* does not take over the body, nor does it dominate the earthly personality.

As a rabbi, I also had serious doubts about the quality of psychic material that would be channeled through an alienated Jew who had allowed himself to be possessed by the spirit of a Nazi war criminal. If "like attracts like," as many esoteric schools teach, then what was really going on here?

According to "New Michael's" own account, the "walk-in" wanted a Jewish body in order to access "cellular memories" of what it is like to be a Jew. I found myself wondering why the soul of Thomas Goettenberg didn't select somebody who knew more about Judaism. Once the "walk-in" took over, "Old Michael's" Jewishness was relegated to bits of nostalgia and a few Yiddish words. As Schuster himself freely admits, "Until recently, it was years since I read a book about Judaism." Ironically, it was my own work which reawakened his "pride and sense of Jewishness."[3]

With these questions in mind, I delved into *Conversations with Adolf Hitler.* I found it to be a very mixed bag. On the one hand, the chapter on "Why the Holocaust?" claims that the souls of the Jews had "volunteered" for their roles before birth, in order to "understand victimization"—a morally repugnant stance to me. But there were also parts of the book which rang true for me. I finally came to the conclusion that, even if Schuster's work was pure fiction, it can still serve as an interesting exercise for examining our own issues surrounding anger, revenge, and forgiveness.

Consider, for example, the "channeled" Hitler's extreme terror at facing his life review after death. Fearing that what he had done to others would now be done to him measure for measure, he apparently walled himself off completely from all help. By using "thought forms" to psychically re-create his underground bunker in Berlin, Hitler was able to retreat into his own madness for forty-four years. Yet even this self-imposed prison could not keep out the inevitable:

> HITLER: The light connecting your world to mine was ever-present in streams of unceasing judgment. I felt judgment by the Jews, the Poles, the Gypsies, the Soviets, the families of those missing, killed, or maimed. This overwhelming judgment on my soul sent me into a whirling path of fear and denial that lasted until, in your terms, the fall of 1989. The space needed to contain my anger and denial was immense. The sheer volume of my repression was enough to frighten anyone in my vicinity. As I continued down this path, I pushed all helping souls away.[4]

I was instantly reminded of the medieval Jewish story about a woman who was possessed by a *dybbuk,* the earthbound soul of a wicked man who had been wandering for over twenty-five years. But how could this be, when Judaism teaches that no soul spends more than a year in Gehenna (purgatory)? The answer, according to the *dybbuk* in the story, was that this applied *only after the soul has actually reached Gehenna,* "For the torment of Gehenna is not even a sixtieth part of what the sinful soul suffers before entering Gehenna."[5]

In the past, I had regarded this tale as mere allegory. Now I was forced to consider the possibility that it might literally be true. After forty-four years in the afterlife, Adolf Hitler, in fear of facing his life review, had only now reached the gates of Gehenna!

In my dream, Hitler was met by three people—the dark-skinned man, the retarded boy, and the old woman in the wheelchair—who came in a van to "take him to the next level." Was that level, in fact, Gehenna? I have always thought of those three people as a *bet din,* the board of three judges which, according to Jewish tradition, conducts our life review in the next world. In Hitler's case, the Heavenly Court was made up of representatives from various groups that he had persecuted—the non-Aryan races, the mentally challenged, the elderly, and the physically handicapped.

My thoughts flashed back to a conference in Olso, Norway, where I was a panelist with Dannion Brinkley, author of the bestselling book, *Saved by the Light.*[6] In that book, Dannion describes his own near-death experience after being struck dead by lightning and then resuscitated. The emotional pain of going through his life review (which depicted him as a selfish bully) brought about a complete change of heart in Dannion. When he came back to this world, he was filled with empathy and deep love for his fellow human beings and has since devoted his life to helping others.

At the Oslo panel discussion, somebody asked, "What about souls like Adolf Hitler? What happens to them?"

Brinkley candidly replied, "When Adolf Hitler faces his life review, he will have to experience all the pain he caused to others as if it were being done to himself. That may not seem fair to us, but it is justice."

At the time, I had agreed with that opinion. Now I was actually reading the "channeled" Hitler's own account of what that life review was really like:

> HITLER: I pulsated with fear and exhaustion and ultimately collapsed to find myself in some sort of hospital. However, coming to my senses was short-lived because great surges of paranoia carried me right back to the fear and exhaustion. This period of hospitalization lasted for what I can only translate as several hundred of earthly years. Understand that time is completely arbitrary. *I was creating more time to contain my insanity*... Not until I had extricated myself from the paranoia did I find it tolerable to remember the 1940s...[7] (Italics are Schuster's)

> The concentration camps haunted me in my hellish afterlife. I often found myself on a table in a concentration camp, with doctors on the verge of dissecting me alive to see what made me tick. This was the agenda of what I was attempting to explore, as my outer nightmare mirrored my inner fears and denial—in *observable* fashion.[8]

According to Mr. Hitler, these scenarios were not inflicted upon him by hellish demons, but were self-created by his growing awareness of the impact of his deeds. Scenes of World War II played over and over, until he was finally able to view them with some level of calm and detachment. He then began to break through his denial and moved into a form of spiritual "group therapy," where he met face-to-face with souls that had suffered in the concentration camps. Many of these souls had arrived in the next world emotionally and spiritually devastated:

HITLER: There are star systems of a spiritual nature that specialize in emotional and physical healing, not of the actual body but of the spirit. The spirit may have suffered when severe emotional blocks were generated around the body, as was common in the concentration camp environment of World War II . . . [9]

The Holocaust itself necessitated planetary systems to care for the souls that so thoroughly lost their will to live that they needed a recharge by the angels of reintegration.[10]

Eventually Mr. Hitler did reach the point of apologizing, although he still had difficulty moving beyond his own pain toward empathizing with the suffering of others. Nevertheless, the apology was a step forward in his recovery:

MICHAEL: What message do you have for Jews today, especially for those who survived your concentration camps?

HITLER: I've feared this question from the onset, but I knew that I would have to face it. As I reflect over and over again on the events of the 1940s, I cringe at the memory of what we did to the Jews and other *untermenschen* (subhumans). I only use this term [now] because it invokes clearest memories. No apology I make can possibly satisfy your readers. I have been looking within myself for what seems an eternity for an answer to this question, an answer that would appease the memories of this horror. I find no solution. I can only offer my apology with the humility of one who has known much pain and self-torture. Now, you may think that self-

> torture cannot balance what was administered in the camps, yet I cannot undo what I created; this is my dilemma and the reason for my stalemate . . .
>
> I do not have an apology for the Jews of today; I have not been able to find the answer within myself. I can only offer my own pain—and the choices I helped frame for the mass consciousness. This may not seem adequate, yet the growth I seek must be the same healing that your world seeks. As I look for love within myself, can you not see that humanity seeks that same love?[11]

From this point on, the book waxes metaphysical. Michael Schuster's spirit guides now join the discussion, to explore the esoteric significance of World War II. A number of "new age" scenarios are presented, involving extraterrestrial influence from the Orion star system, an interplanetary "karmic blow-out" to clear centuries of pent-up feelings on earth, and a parallel earth where the Holocaust did not happen in such severity. The past, according to Mr. Hitler, is very flexible and can be changed.

As science fiction, these scenarios would make fascinating plots for "alternate histories." But if this is really what the soul of Hitler believes, then he still has a long way to go toward repentance. Having finally faced up to his denial and admitted that he caused enormous pain and suffering to millions of people, he now takes refuge in the "bargaining" stage of recovery. Over and over, the "channeled" Hitler desperately searches for a trade-off that will somehow make the abuse seem OK. There are no victims, we are told repeatedly, because everyone "volunteered" for their roles before incarnating on the earth plane. And once they were here, they didn't really feel the pain in the camps, because they were in "altered states of consciousness" at the time.[12]

If such rationalizations were to show up in a therapy group for abusers, we would immediately challenge them. Unfortunately, when it comes to psychically channeled material, many people do not question the quality of what comes through. But being dead does not automatically make a soul all-knowing or even wise. What Hitler offers us here are the excuses of a sociopath. What abuser has not claimed that "she really wanted it," and that the victim either "did not feel anything" or "actually enjoyed the pain"?

After reading *Conversations*, a chilling possibility continued to linger in my mind. During the past few years, there has been a proliferation of esoteric material which claims that the Jews "chose the Holocaust" or that it was some kind of "earth cleansing"—a term that is too close to "ethnic cleansing" for my comfort. Today I have deep concerns about the esoteric source(s) of these ideas. Could it be that since the time when Hitler's soul "awakened" in 1989, the psychics have been tuning into his "bargaining stage" mentality and mistaking it for divine inspiration?

If, as Michael Schuster believes, my dream was more than a dream, then my willingness to embrace Adolf might well have had a positive effect upon his soul. If that is true, then it was because I allowed myself to empathize—literally *to feel with*—the abuse that he suffered in his childhood. For me, that empathy led to forgiveness—but that was only the beginning of the process for Hitler. In order for him to heal the pain he has caused to others, he must acknowledge its existence, neither wishing it away through denial nor attempting to bargain it into a "learning experience" for the victims. In the interests of planetary healing, I sincerely pray that the soul of Hitler—wherever it may now be—will one day come to realize this and complete the cycle of repentance.

Appendix C:

Edgar Cayce on the Holocaust

by Rabbi Yonassan Gershom

In July 1993, I was invited to speak on reincarnation and the Holocaust at a symposium sponsored by the Association for Research and Enlightenment, Inc. (A.R.E.), in Virginia Beach, Virginia.[1] While participating in this conference, I was approached by several individuals, both Jewish and Christian, who had each heard the same disturbing rumor. According to "new age" hearsay, the psychic Edgar Cayce had attributed the suffering of the Jews during the Holocaust to past-life karma. This karma, in turn, was supposedly rooted in "something the Jews did in biblical times."

Understandably, this rumor was upsetting to these gentle seekers. Not only did it defame Edgar Cayce, it also blamed the victims for Nazi war crimes. Upon further inquiry, however, nobody seemed to know just what this "biblical karma" was supposed to be, nor did anyone have a specific reference from the Cayce material itself. Everyone had just "heard it from somebody else." Like rumors often do, this one went round and round to nowhere.

As a rabbi who writes about reincarnation, I, too, have heard this "blame the victim" theory about Nazi atrocities. In fact, my files are filled with letters from self-appointed experts setting me straight on the "true meaning" of the Holocaust. Precisely because the issue of "Jewish karma" has been raised so many times before, the questions posed to me in Virginia Beach came as no big surprise.

This time, however, I was right there at the A.R.E. headquarters, with direct access to the more than 14,000 Edgar Cayce readings on file, along with a vast quantity of follow-up reports. Therefore, I decided to take the bull by the horns and research the Cayce material for myself. I was determined to find out what, if anything, the readings actually said about the suffering of the Jews during World War II.

Like so many rumors, this one turned out to be a garbled mixture of fact and fiction. Yes, Cayce did mention a few biblical passages that could be interpreted as references to the Holocaust. But no, these same verses do not necessarily say that the Holocaust was a karmic payback. Quite the contrary. I believe that Cayce was referring to *the return of the Jews to the land of Israel!* If I am correct, then this is a prophecy fulfilled, which was generally overlooked by the previous generation of scholars!

To understand how I came to this startling conclusion, which stands the "karmic payback" rumor on its head, I invite you to join me in a re-creation of my scholarly detective work. In this essay, we will follow a fascinating trail of clues, sometimes obvious and sometimes hidden, in order to solve this esoteric mystery.

Right from the beginning, I discovered that very few Cayce readings directly mention Jews or the Holocaust at all. In fact, most of the questions about Nazi Germany were focused on politics and economics. We must remember that, just prior to World War II, the United States and Europe were still recovering from the Great Depression. At the same time, the Russian Revolution of 1917 was fresh in the public mind, with Communism on the rise, both at home and abroad. Understandably, many of Cayce's clients were very concerned about how the political situation in Europe would affect their business investments.[2]

When I examined the readings from this period, I quickly saw that the rise of Adolf Hitler, with his appointment as Chancellor of Germany in 1933, was high on the list of concerns. On the one hand, Hitler was bringing economic recovery to Europe. But on the other hand, the dark side of the Nazi regime was already revealing itself, with rising militarism, tight control of the press, and persecution of Jews and other minorities.

The questions posed to Cayce during these years clearly reflect the fear and confusion which permeated the Western world at that time: Was it safe to invest in Europe? Would Hitler remain in power? Would there be war? Would the United States become involved?

On November 4, 1933, a small group of people gathered in Staten Island, New York, to obtain a psychic reading from Cayce on "the political situation that exists in Germany proper today, analyzing the policies of the present ruler [Hitler]."[3] This "Hitler reading," as I will call it here, proved to be one of those cases where, for reasons we can only guess at, the sleeping Cayce was pointed in the wrong direction.

The Hitler reading began accurately enough, describing how the negative impact of the Treaty of Versailles had demoralized the German people, paving the way for the rise of Nazism. Most historians today would agree with this analysis.[4] But then the Hitler reading veered off target. What came through next was a very optimistic picture of Hitler's regime, which portrayed him as a "psychically led" leader, who was "called for a purpose." If he avoided imperialism, the readings said, Hitler's policies would supposedly "make for the light to the world," and eventually lead to "a new ideal in the hearts, in the minds of the people." On the political front, Adolf Hitler could actually bring better relationships between France and Germany. Rumors of war, the reading clearly stated, were only propaganda.

Nowadays, the most casual student of history can easily recognize that this part of the Hitler reading was dead wrong. As it was being channeled, one can only hope that there were people in the room who were shocked by what was coming through Cayce. But the questions continued: "Is Hitler's idea of one party the best for Germany?" "Why is it that apparently Hitler is making a mistake in initiating policies that seem to be antagonizing the world?" "Analyze Hitler's attitude towards the Jews."

Had I been there, I would have asked, "How can a man of God be channeling a positive reading about Hitler in the first place?" The same perplexing question is still posed among thoughtful students of the Cayce readings today. The answer, I believe, lies in the peculiar circumstances surrounding the reading itself.

As has been amply demonstrated throughout the Cayce material, the exact wording of the questions was very important. So was the client's reason for requesting the information. If the question was too vague or the seeker's motive was not pure, then the quality of the material received could be seriously affected. Cayce himself described the problem this way:

> The attempt then to interpret or to read such [psychic] records depends much upon the attitude,

> the desire of the individual or soul-entity seeking to know same. Yet the very desire of such may be overshadowed by the individuality of an entity, as to cause deflections from that which might be an interpretation for constructive influences . . .
>
> For thoughts are things, and as they run, so are the impressions made upon what we call time and space. Hence often there is confusion . . . in differentiating between that which was the thought of an individual and that which was the actual activity.[5]

Was the Hitler reading a result of poor psychic attunement? Did unclear wording invoke ambiguous material that was later misunderstood? In my opinion, the answer to both questions is "yes." For example, when asked to "Analyze Hitler's attitude towards the Jews," the sleeping Cayce replied:

> When the *character* of those that have received, in a manner, their dictations—or the dictates of the activity of the director in affairs—is considered, then it will be understood how that this is but that diction which was given of old; and how that those peoples though they *were* called—have wandered far afield, and their rebelliousness and their seeking into the affairs of *others* has rather brought *them* into *their* present position.[6]

Notice how Cayce answered the exact question put to him—by analyzing *Hitler's* attitude! Taken out of context, this passage could easily appear to be blaming the Jews for the Holocaust.[7] But is this a "universal truth" about karma or merely a summary of Hitler's own twisted beliefs? To address this question, we must now turn to the next clue in our little mystery: For whom was the Hitler reading actually given?

According to the A.R.E. records, the idea for the Hitler reading was suggested by another Cayce reading, given on the previous day, for a Mr. [378].[8] This same [378] was a blatant anti-Semite, who later moved with his family to Nazi Germany in April of 1938. In December 1938, he wrote a long letter to Cayce from Munich, praising Hitler's regime and claiming that any negative reports against Hitler were nothing more than "a malicious Jewish campaign to injure German trade."[9]

Mr. [378] was also very pleased with the way that Hitler was handling "the Jewish question." He urged the United States to follow the example set by Hitler, who "did no more than Christ did in the Temple"—apparently a reference to how Jesus overturned the tables of the money-changers. This allusion is all the more ominous when we realize that [378] wrote this *after Kristallnacht,* the infamous "Night of Broken Glass," when the Nazis smashed, burned, and looted hundreds of Jewish-owned businesses.

Such was the man whose personal reading had suggested a more general reading on Hitler. Did this psychic linkage somehow throw the Hitler reading off track? Were [378]'s pro-Nazi thoughts affecting Cayce's consciousness while he was channeling? I think yes. It is possible that Cayce was actually reading [378]'s mind, rather than receiving the information from a higher spiritual source. In my opinion, it was a case of garbage in, garbage out.

From [378]'s perspective, however, the Hitler reading must have seemed like divine confirmation of his own Nazi beliefs. We must keep in mind that the Nazis were very interested in "the occult" and often misused psychic teachings for their own ends. According to Dusty

Sklar in *The Nazis and the Occult,* many esoteric circles of that time were espousing bizarre nineteenth-century ideas about human evolution, combined with ancient mythology. Some of these pseudo-scientific theories blamed "the Jews" for every evil on the face of the earth, including the primordial Fall from spiritual to material existence. "German anti-Semitism," writes Sklar, "was fed by an underground stream of secret cults running like a sewer beneath Vienna and other cultural centers."[10]

In America, too, anti-Semitism ran rampant. Before the United States entered the war in 1942, Adolf Hitler had many American sympathizers, even among so-called "good Christians."[11] Given this atmosphere, I think we can safely assume that [378]'s Nazi cronies were delighted to think that their ideas were "confirmed" by a credible psychic like Edgar Cayce. No doubt they told others, who told others, who told others—to the point that a very garbled "oral tradition" about "negative Jewish karma" continues to circulate in the name of Cayce to this day.

In all fairness, we must be very clear that Cayce himself was not a Nazi, nor am I accusing him personally of anti-Semitism. In the waking state, Edgar Cayce was a man of good will, and the readings he channeled as "the sleeping prophet" clearly affirmed the value of all human life. In addition, Cayce counted a number of Jews among his closest friends and supporters. It is for this very reason that we must carefully examine this issue of "Jewish karma," in order to save the wheat and avoid perpetuating the chaff.

But even if we were to take the Hitler reading at face value as a judgment against the Jews (which I most certainly do not!), nowhere does it advocate genocide, nor does it refer to concentration camps. Instead, immediately after examining Hitler's attitude toward the Jews, the reading goes on to reference a biblical prophecy:

> Read they [the Jews?] not that which has been given? "When ye forsake my ways ye shall be scattered, ye shall be without those things that would bring ye into the knowledge—until that time is fulfilled."
>
> Hence the attitude [of Hitler?] that is assumed is rather a fulfillment of that prophecy that has been made, *and is the beginning of the return that must come throughout the earth.*[12] (Brackets and italics mine.)

Notice how the reading shifts away from Hitler's anti-Semitism and moves toward the fulfillment of a prophecy about "the beginning of the return." When I first read this passage, I was immediately reminded of the words of Moses to the Jewish people in the biblical book of Deuteronomy:

> He (God) will gather you again from the countries where He has scattered you. Even though He were to banish you to the four corners of the world, the Lord (YHVH) your God *will gather you from there; from there He will fetch you home.*[13] (Italics mine)

In Edgar Cayce's day, there were both Jews and Christians who saw World War II as "the time of the end" and were expecting the fulfillment of biblical prophecies about the "Great Return." For Christians, this expectation was connected with the Second Coming of Christ. For Jews, the same prophecy meant the coming of the Messianic Age, when Jews would return to the Holy Land, and the entire world would live in peace. Many of the Cayce readings from that period suggest that World War II was Armageddon, the last battle between good and evil.[14]

According to Rabbi Zalman Schachter, who escaped the Holocaust in the 1940s, there was a strong messianic fervor in the Hasidic communities of that time, in both Europe and America:

> In 1943 the [sixth] Lubovitcher Rebbe [Joseph I. Schneerson, died 1950] published several lessons about how the Messiah was coming soon. The exile *[golus]* was burning down, the Rebbe said, and that's what was going on in Europe. It was *mechevalei moschiach*, the "birth pangs of the Messiah . . .
>
> "Always everybody is saying that we Jews didn't know about it [the genocide]. How could we not know? Go to the *London Jewish Chronicle* and look at the headlines for those years: '10,000 Jews killed in Biastolok' . . . Those headlines were scary. So the Messiah was expected very soon—it's all a matter of public record in Lubovitch circles."[15]

Back in 1933, the seekers who were present when Cayce channeled the Hitler reading were also aware of the persecution of Jews in Europe, as indicated by this exchange:

> Q. What should become of the Jews?
>
> A. They should hearken to that call given of old. Their gathering together in their *own* land.[16]

Does this answer sound like a karmic payback? Does it foretell a Holocaust? No, it does not. Instead, the reading refers us to the fulfillment of a well-known biblical promise to the Jewish people: the return to their ancestral homeland!

Of course, if we were to rely on the Hitler reading alone to draw this conclusion, we would be skating on very thin ice. Fortunately, this is not the only place where Cayce spoke of the Jews returning to Palestine. We go now to the 257 series of readings, given for a Jewish sales manager who was a longtime associate member of A.R.E. Over a period of many years, Mr. [257] received literally hundreds of readings, which he carefully followed. In addition to business advice, [257] also sought answers of a more philosophical nature. His reading for September 25, 1939, contains the following exchange about World War II:

> Q. For what real purpose is the present war?
> A. Read in Daniel, the last two chapters, and see; also the 31st of Deuteronomy—and we will see.[17]

When I looked up the last two chapters in the Book of Daniel, I found that they were prophecies about the "last days." At that time, according to the Bible, a Hitler-like king would arise and "exalt and magnify himself above every god, and against the God of gods he will utter monstrous blasphemies . . . To no god will he pay heed, but will exalt himself above them all."[18] This same tyrant would also persecute "the people who do know their God."

Space here does not permit a verse-by-verse analysis of Daniel 11 and 12, but I would like to suggest a general mode of interpretation. In order to follow my reasoning here, it is important to remember that the entire Old Testament—including the Book of Daniel—is originally Jewish. When Jews read Daniel's prophecies about "the last days," they do not see them as "Christian" references to the "Second Coming of Christ." Instead, these passages are interpreted as the words of a Jewish prophet speaking to his own people, *the Jews who are suffering in exile.*

As we have already learned, Mr. [257]—the man who asked about the "real purpose" of this war—was himself Jewish. Therefore, it is reasonable to assume that the readings would speak to him in the context of his own religion. And sure enough, if we examine the Book of Daniel through Jewish eyes, by reading "the people" as "the Jews in exile," these passages come alive when compared with the Holocaust:

> He [the wicked king] will turn and vent his fury against the Holy Covenant . . . They will set up the abominable thing which causes desolation . . . And such as do wickedly against the Covenant shall corrupt by flatteries; but the people that know their God shall be strong and do exploits (or fight back). And they that understand among the people shall instruct many; yet they shall fall by the sword, by flame, by captivity, and by spoil for many days.[19]

In Jewish parlance, any reference to "the Covenant" automatically refers to the Revelation at Mt. Sinai and the eternal pledge of loyalty between God and the Jewish people.[20] Seen in this context, Adolf Hitler did "do wickedly against the Covenant" by reviling everyone and everything that was Jewish. He also "corrupted" the German people "by flatteries," claiming that they were a "master race," destined to rule the world.

The "abominable thing which causes desolation" mentioned by Daniel is usually interpreted as some type of idolatry. But it could also refer to the concentration camps, where millions of people were burned on the satanic altar of Nazi madness. The prophecy then continues:

> And some of them of understanding shall fall, to

> try [or test] them, and to purge, and to make them white [purified], even to the time of the end; because it is yet for a time appointed.[21]

Again, we must remember that when Jews read these verses, they see them as references to Jewish martyrs. Historically, there are numerous eyewitness accounts of Hasidic rabbis who urged their followers to accept the martyr's death as a form of purification, both personal and collective. For example, Rabbi Israel Shapiro, the Hasidic Rebbe of Grodzisk, Poland, drew upon this imagery in Daniel when he told his followers in the Treblinka concentration camp:

> These, our sufferings, are meant to precede the coming of the Messiah. If it was decreed that we should be the victims of the Messianic throes, that we should go up in flames to herald the redemption, then we should consider ourselves fortunate to have this privilege. Our ashes will serve to cleanse the people of Israel who will remain, and so our deaths will hasten the day when the Messiah will appear.[22]

According to eyewitness reports, Rabbi Shapiro and his Hasidim walked into the gas chambers with heads held high, singing the words of Maimonides: "I believe with perfect faith in the coming of the Messiah, and though he may tarry, yet will I believe . . . " Of course, not every Holocaust victim died with such consciousness. But "some of them of understanding" definitely did, and "some" is what the prophecy says.

The second biblical section mentioned in Mr. [257]'s reading was Deuteronomy 31, which opens with the deathbed statement of Moses. The old prophet is now 120 years old, and God has ordered him not to cross over the

Jordan River. Therefore, Moses is turning over the leadership to Joshua, with clear instructions: "Be strong and of good courage, for you must go with this people unto the land which the Lord has sworn unto their ancestors to give them, and you shall cause them to possess it."[23]

Over the years, a number of people have cited this reference to me as proof that the Israelite battles with the Canaanites are the karmic source for the deaths of Jews in Nazi Germany. According to this theory, the people who were killed by Joshua's army came back to wreak revenge. If we interpret karma as mere tit for tat, then this argument might work. But I seriously question whether this is what Cayce really intended, for a number of reasons.

First of all, the Cayce readings claim that Joshua and Jesus were the same soul, an entity known as "Amilius" in the pre-existent spirit world.[24] Both the waking Cayce and the sleeping Cayce deeply revered Jesus as a perfect spiritual master, the bearer of the Christ Light. Within the context of these beliefs, it would not be consistent for Cayce to claim that Joshua—the soul that would become Jesus—had misled the Jews into such negative karma that it resulted in the deaths of millions 3,000 years later!

In fact, the waking Cayce saw Joshua as a righteous warrior who fought in the service of God. According to Robert Krajenke, Edgar Cayce once compared Joshua's battles to the conquest of the American Indians by the Europeans, in order to create "a Christian nation."[25] Although we may shudder at this outdated view of history, we must remember that "manifest destiny" was a common belief in Cayce's day. Far from seeing the invasion of Canaan as a karmic liability, Cayce saw Joshua's battles as divinely guided for a greater purpose.

In addition, we must also ask: If the reading in question were making a karmic connection between World War II and the Joshua battles, wouldn't it make more sense to refer directly to the book of Joshua, where the battles take place? Why take us, instead, to the deathbed of Moses?

In my opinion, Cayce's reference to Deuteronomy was really a prediction about the new state of Israel, couched in a metaphor that was not properly understood back in the 1930s. With historical hindsight, we can now see the analogy more clearly: The old generation of Jews in Europe, symbolized by "Moses in the wilderness," was coming to an end. And like Moses, many of the sages from the Holocaust generation would not live to see the promised ingathering. But the new "Joshua" generation would "be strong and of good courage." They would "cross over Jordan" and "possess the land"—as actually happened with the founding of the State of Israel in 1948.

The very fact that Cayce referenced the last chapters of Daniel and Deuteronomy to *a Jewish seeker* suggests, to me at least, that the "real purpose" of this war is connected with *the end of the 2,000-year-old exile!* Of course, individual souls may have chosen to utilize the Holocaust or the war itself as a way to work out personal karma. That happens in any event. But for the Jewish people on the collective level, World War II was *mechevalai moschiach,* the "birth pangs of Messiah"—the pain and suffering that always comes when something new is born into the world.

Within the mainstream Jewish community today, the idea that "out of the ashes of Auschwitz arose the phoenix of Israel" is commonly accepted theology. But, on the other hand, current Israeli society is hardly the glorious utopia foretold by biblical prophecy. Many Jews, including myself, see the militant nationalism of Israeli society as contrary to both the law and the spirit of the Torah, and the assassination in 1996 of Prime Minister Yitzchak Rabin (may his name be remembered for a blessing) is a sad reminder of how far we have yet to go.[26] How, then, can I accept the idea that the return to Israel was a fulfillment of biblical prophecy?

I have puzzled over this question for many years. Then one day, while doing the research for this essay, I found a beautiful teaching by Rabbi Abraham Isaac Kook, also known as Rav (master scholar) Kook, the first Chief Rabbi of Israel. Rav Kook once compared the establishment of modern Israel to the original process of erecting the Holy Temple in Jerusalem. While the construction crew was putting up the building, Rav Kook explained, anybody could walk anywhere on the Temple site. But once the Temple was completed and formally dedicated to God, then only the High Priest could enter the Holy of Holies. In the same way, the coarse events surrounding the birth of the state of Israel are not the final product, but only the fallible work of ordinary people, who are still in the process of "building the sanctuary."[27]

What is true for a struggling young nation is also true for our planet as a whole. All of us are like those Temple construction workers, struggling to rebuild a sanctuary from the smoldering ashes. Whether we see it as prophecy or sociology, World War II did mark the "end of the world" as our ancestors knew it, and the aftermath has propelled us into a new age of awareness. At the same time, we are still cleaning up the rubble in the global village, and the process of *tikkun olam*—repairing the world—is far from over. Each of us, Jew and Gentile alike, still has much work to do. Therefore, let us dedicate ourselves to planetary healing, each in our own way, so that the promised age of messianic peace may arise, at last, like a phoenix from the ashes.

Notes

Introduction

1. See Talmud, Shabbat 67a. To this day, even very Orthodox Jews will violate the Sabbath in a medical emergency and will take medications derived from nonkosher species (such as swine or horse serum), when no other alternatives are available. From a Jewish standpoint, there is no special virtue in refusing medical treatment on religious grounds.

2. Shapiro, Amy, book review, *Journal of Regression Therapy,* Fall 1994, pp. 103-104.

3. Rifkin, Ira, "Come Again? Jewish speakers at a Towson conference on reincarnation say recalling past lives can make this one better," *Baltimore Jewish Times,* October 22, 1993.

4. *Ibid.* In his second book, *Through Time into Healing* (Simon and Schuster, New York, 1992), Dr. Weiss cites a case of a woman who remembers dying in a Nazi concentration camp (pp. 115-117). Both Dr. Weiss and I were involved in the case of Taylor Sammons, whose story was featured on the network TV program, *Sightings* (Paramount 1995).

5. Scholem, Gershom G., *Major Trends in Jewish Mysticism,* Schocken Books, Inc., New York, 1946, pp. 16-17.

6. *Op. cit.,* Rifkin.

7. Wiesel, Eli, "The Death of My Father," included in Riemer, Jack, *Jewish Reflections on Death,* Schocken Books, Inc., New York, 1978, p. 38.

Chapter One

"The Healer Heals Herself" by Abbye Silverstein

1. "G-d" is a traditional Jewish way of writing "God." According to Jewish law, there are ten sacred Hebrew Names for the Creator which, once written, may never be erased or destroyed. Although technically this refers to the specific Names as written with Hebrew letters, many Orthodox Jews extend this respect to translations as well. In addition, some non-Orthodox Jews also use "G-d" to distinguish between the One G-d of Judaism and the "gods" of other religions.

2. Student dissidents: In the early days of the Third Reich, there were a number of such movements, loosely designated as "Edelweiss Pirates," because they met under the cover of Alpine hiking trips and used the edelweiss flower as their symbol. (Taylor, James, and Shaw, Warren, *The Third Reich Almanac,* Pharos Books, New York, 1987, p. 103.) The song "Edelweiss" in the Broadway musical, *The Sound of Music,* is a literary reference to this anti-Nazi protest.

3. This imagery is consistent with what many Jews of that time might have expected the gates of Heaven to be like. During the late nineteenth and early twentieth century, Ellis Island was the place in New York Harbor where new immigrants were screened. The United Jewish Appeal is a social services agency which extends aid to refugees. Compare the story of "Beverly" in *Beyond the Ashes,* who also saw Jews standing in long lines, waiting to get into Heaven (pp. 20-23).

4. See Appendix A.

Chapter Two

"The Clock" by Bruce Whittier

1. Under hypnosis as "Stefan," Bruce recorded a sample of this language. The words appear to be meaningless, but the sound does resemble Hebrew (not Yiddish), as if he were imitating something poorly learned. "Stefan" also said that he did not understand the meaning of the prayers, but attended synagogue "three times a week" on a regular basis. This is an important detail that most non-Jews would not know. Although services are held daily, the Torah scroll is only read on Monday, Thursday, and the Sabbath—three times a week—and many Jews go only on those days.

"Stefan" also described his mother buying two loaves of "round bread" for the Sabbath. Unfortunately, the hypnotist, who is not familiar with Jewish customs, misunderstood this as "brown bread" and did not ask for further details. Sabbath bread is usually braided, but round loaves are also used, especially on Rosh Hashanah.

The hypnotist also threw his subject off track by asking him to recall the beginning of the Sabbath day "early in the morning." In fact, the Jewish Sabbath begins at sundown on Friday, not Saturday morning. Nevertheless, "Stefan" dutifully followed instructions, first describing how he studied Hebrew with his father—a plausible morning activity—then backtracking to the "beginning of the Sabbath" with breaking the round loaves.

2. Kim and George McAdoo, "The Time Travelers," 112 Sherri Lane, Lower Sackville, Nova Scotia, B4G 1A8, Canada.

3. When asked about his name in the previous life, Bruce replied "Steven" in English. But later, when he

was "in character" quoting his mother from that life, he said, "Stefan" as in Dutch. He did the same with his wife's name, first calling her "Helen" as in English, but later referring to her as "eh-LENN," which we chose to render as "Helene." When asked to spell his last name, Horwitz, he ended with a "zet" rather than a "zee" as in English. In this life, he does not know Dutch or German.

4. According to Bruce, the horns were not metallic, but very deep-sounding and primitive, like "Tibetan horns." Was "Stefan" hearing the *shofar,* a sacred ram's horn which, according to Jewish tradition, is sounded on the Day of Judgment? Bruce was also puzzled that the celestial light was blue, when similar accounts describe a golden light. Here again, we have a possible Jewish connection. The color yellow has a negative connotation for Jews, because of the yellow badges worn during the Holocaust. On the other hand, blue is a spiritual color to most Jews.

Chapter Three

"Flashbacks in Vienna" by Lena-Marie Broman

1. That is, from a previous incarnation. Broman added, "She was now around seventy years old, so it was quite possible that I knew her from my last life." It is also interesting that the woman kept staring. Did she, on some level, also recognize "Anna-Maria" from the past life?

2. Whether Broman spent time at this location in the other life is not clear. The Red Cross buses in the vision suggest that she may have been "seeing" a scene from a refugee camp. The location on the west coast of Sweden also fits this possibility, because this is directly across the North Sea from Denmark. In 1943, in one of the most daring rescue operations of

the war, Danish sea captains and fishermen smuggled Danish Jews across the sea to safety in Sweden. Throughout the war, this underground activity continued. (See Gilbert, Martin, *Holocaust: A History of the Jews of Europe During the Second World War*, Henry Holt & Company, New York, 1985, p. 614.)

3. The Nuremberg Laws, passed by the Nazis in 1935, forbade marriage between Jews and Germans and declared marriages conducted "in defiance of this law" to be invalid. Sexual intercourse outside of marriage was also forbidden between Jews and Germans, in the name of "racial purity." Lena-Marie, as "Anna-Maria Kellerman," was Jewish in her previous life, while Jürg was German. Therefore, little Heinz, the child of their union, was "forbidden fruit."

4. Dr. Göran Grip: a Swedish medical doctor and author of *Everything Exists*, published in Sweden in the fall of 1994. He has also translated into Swedish many important books in the field of consciousness research.

5. In their presentation at the 1994 "Reincarnation and Rebirth" symposium in Oslo, Norway, Broman and Grip described other details of the camp which she had seen in her past-life memories. These are described in their new book, soon to be published by Forum Press (Stockholm, Sweden). One particularly impressive detail was Broman's description of a cleared field and a slope at Buchenwald, which she remembered vividly from her previous life. However, when she returned to the site in this life, no such view existed. Broman was puzzled by this, until she remembered that over fifty years had passed. Where there once was a field, large trees now stood. After walking down the forest path, she and Dr. Grip came to an opening—and there was the very same view from her

past life! She had "seen" the landscape around Buchenwald, not as it is now, but as it had been when the camp was in operation—before Lena-Marie Broman was even born!

6. As with her mental pictures of Buchenwald, she remembered Vienna as it had been in that lifetime, not as it is today. In one case, where a building had been remodeled, the door was in the "wrong" place. Once inside, they could see, from the position of the stairwell, how the door used to be—in the "right" place after all!

7. Jews, who were forced to wear a yellow star on their outer clothing, were constant targets for abuse and harassment. In addition, there were curfews and other restrictions, including rules about when and where Jewish children could be on the streets. Even if one escaped personal injury, there were constant sights of beatings, arrests, and other persecutions. This was the horror that "Anna-Maria" sought to avoid by using the well-remembered shortcut.

8. This refers to the Cathedral of St. Stephen's, a major landmark in the center of Old Vienna. In both lives, the conspicuous dome of this building helped her to orient herself within the city.

Chapter Four

"Hands from the Holocaust" by David R. Moffatt

1. Prior to the Holocaust, Lodz was a major center of Jewish learning. At times during its history, the Jewish population of Lodz made up a third or more of the total population. When Hitler invaded Poland in 1939, there were an estimated 233,000 Jews living in Lodz. Source: Wiesenthal, Simon, *Every Day Remembrance Day,* Henry Holt and Company, New York, 1987, p. 202.

2. The anti-Semitic graffiti was apparently added

by tourists. Moffatt also told me that he saw the Star of David in a hangman's noose scrawled on walls throughout Poland during his visit.

3. Moffatt also stated that he had never had such a problem with this camera in the past, and that it had been professionally recalibrated and tested just prior to departing for Poland. There have been no problems with it since.

4. I personally examined these photos, which were as described. In addition, Moffatt had similar underexposure problems while photographing the Holocaust memorial in the city of Lodz, using a different camera. That camera, too, now works fine.

5. Although the dream clearly has symbolic elements, it does bear some resemblance to the infamous "standing cells" of Birkenau, which were in a wooden building. See Marcia Hollabaugh's story ("More Than a Fairy Tale"), where these cells were "seen" in more detail.

Chapter Five
"The White Rose" by Judith Hart

1. "The White Rose" was organized in 1939 at Munich University by students Hans and Sophie Scholl, who distributed anti-Hitlerite pamphlets calling for democracy, restoration of social justice, and decentralization of the government. See Scholl, Inge, *The White Rose*, Munich 1942-'43, translated by Arthur Schultz, Wesleyan University Press, 1983.

Chapter Six
"More Than a Fairy Tale" by Marcia Hollabaugh

1. The image of a "factory" belching pollution into the sky appears frequently in Holocaust past-life memories. Regarding architecture at Auschwitz-

Birkenau, Charles Lawless writes, "Deceptive with their steep roofs, dormer windows, stout chimneys, and tasteful landscaping, these one-story brick structures deliberately resembled modern German industrial buildings." (Lawless, Charles, *And God Cried: The Holocaust Remembered,* Wieser & Wieser, Inc., New York, 1994, p. 129)

2. Both Pittsburgh and the area around Auschwitz have this type of forest, which could account for the dream beginning on a familiar path near her home and leading to memories of another life.

3. In the two largest complexes at Birkenau, the gas chambers were underground and would seem like a "maze" or "cave" from a child's perspective. (A scale model of such a complex can be seen at the United States Holocaust Memorial Museum in Washington, D.C.) Although Hollabaugh saw one body per "cave," in fact, three or more corpses were sometimes put into each oven at once for more efficient cremation (*op. cit.,* Lawless, pp. 129-130).

4. Hollabaugh's lack of exposure to Judaism is also obvious from the imagery in the temple dream, which is more like a church than a synagogue. A Jewish place of worship does not usually have a Star of David hanging in front like a cross in a church, nor does it have an altar. Instead, there is an Ark (cabinet) built into the wall, where the Torah scrolls are kept. Most Orthodox congregations do not use a choir in the synagogue, although sacred music for all-male choirs does exist. Many Reform and Conservative congregations do use a choir, with both male and female voices.

5. The theory of "cellular memories" suggests that our experiences are somehow encoded into our genes, then passed on to our children. In the case of the woman who converted to Judaism, this would be

theoretically possible, because she is a direct descendant of the "Yiddish-speaking" (and presumably Jewish) grandmother. In the case of Marcia Hollabaugh, however, "cellular memories of Auschwitz" do not make sense, because her parents were alive in America at the time of the Holocaust, and she has no ancestors who died at Auschwitz. She later decided that reincarnation is a better explanation. (See also Appendix A for a discussion of cases where non-Jews are the reincarnation of a "lost" Jewish ancestor.)

6. *Auschwitz: A History in Photographs,* published for the Auschwitz-Birkenau State Museum, Warsaw, by Indiana University Press, 1993.

7. Hollabaugh later found another uncanny reference to the "barbershop poles." On pages 266-267 of *Auschwitz: A History in Photographs,* there is a large photo of the western entrance to Auschwitz with the infamous *Arbeit Macht Frei* ("Work shall make you free") gate. On either side of this gate are two diagonally striped poles which do, indeed, resemble barbershop poles. They even have balls on top!

Chapter Seven

"Each One Has a Name" by Diana Lubarsky

1. Holocaust denial was not limited to marginally involved Jews. Harvard law professor Alan Dershowitz, who grew up as an Orthodox Jew in Brooklyn, writes: "Although I recalled my father's map [of Europe] and the influx of displaced persons in my neighborhood, the Jewish community of my school years had experienced collective amnesia about the Holocaust. It was never mentioned in yeshiva, in Jewish [summer] camp, in discussions among friends, even in the synagogue . . . The tragedy was too recent, too painful, too evocative of guilt." (Dershowitz, Alan M., *Chutzpah,*

Little, Brown, and Company, Boston 1991, p. 49)

2. Moldover, Sheila, "She remembers what she never saw," *The Yorktowner,* Yorktown Heights, New York, Vol. XII, No. 6, May-June 1978, p. 38.

3. *Ibid.*

4. Roman Vishniac was born in St. Petersburg in 1897 and was educated at the universities of Moscow and Berlin. In 1938, just before the Nazis invaded Poland, Vishniac toured Eastern Europe, producing what is probably the last set of photographs depicting a lost epoch. His work *Polish Jews: A Pictorial Record* (Schocken Books, 1947) is now a classic.

5. The book was *Roman Vishniac,* Grossman Publishers, New York, 1974. The photo of the woman appears on page 92.

6. Unfortunately, Roman Vishniac has passed away, so this question remains a mystery. But there is no question that the sculptures moved him deeply. In 1985, he visited Lubarsky's home, where he broke down and cried over the sculpture, "Empty Spaces." He autographed her copy of his book, *A Vanished World,* with these words: "To Diana, the Holocaust artist who understands and feels. I thought about all this that happened later. I was trembling, being afraid that it could happen. Diana knows how to produce great sculptures of [the] Holocaust. I never saw such beautiful sculptures comparing with *Guernica*—you will not believe [it] today—I know it for sure. Diana is greater than Picasso."

7. See *Holocaust,* Yad Vashem, Jerusalem 1977, pp. 70-71. In October 1995, I had the opportunity to view the photo and the sculpture side-by-side. The resemblance is remarkable.

Chapter Eight

"Say Kaddish for Us" by Sigrid Dreyfuss-Manelis

1. "Mayflower Jews": Although there were apparently no Jews aboard the actual *Mayflower,* the next ship to arrive in Plymouth Rock, the *Fortune,* carried at least one "Hebrew Pilgrim" named Moses Simonson. His grandson married Sarah Standish, granddaughter of John Alden and Miles Standish, Puritans who arrived aboard the *Mayflower.* Jews also settled in New Amsterdam [now Manhattan] as early as 1654 (Sharfman, Harold I., *Jews on the Frontier,* Henry Regnery Company, Chicago, 1977, p. 73).

2. Fräulein Neilah: A reference to the Neilah service which ends the Yom Kippur (Day of Atonement) prayers after sunset. In the symbolism of the Jewish liturgy, Neilah is when "the decree is sealed" by God for the coming year regarding who shall live and who shall die—an appropriate code for impending death.

3. British-born Ambrose Worrall (1899-1972) and his American-born wife Olga (1906-1985) were both gifted clairvoyants and psychic healers whose work is well documented. During her lifetime, Olga Worrall's healing abilities were scientifically investigated by physicians, parapsychologists, and others, including nuclear physicist Elizabeth Rauschner and biophysicist Beverly Rubik. In 1979, Olga also underwent parapsychological experiments at the University of California in Berkeley to study her unusual abilities (Guiley, Rosemary Ellen, *Harper's Encyclopedia of Mystical and Paranormal Experience,* HarperCollins, New York, 1991, pp. 650-653).

Chapter Nine
"I Remember" by Carole Louie

1. As is well known, the Christian Easter story took place during the week of Passover, and the outer forms of some Jewish rituals were carried over by the early churches. For example, the white tablecloth and two candles, the unleavened bread and wine, the Pascal lamb, and the story of the Exodus are all originally from the Jewish Passover Seder. However, within the Jewish worldview the ceremonial foods remain simply foods to be eaten in the service of God, but not transsubstantiated as with the Catholic host. The Christian idea of "Holy Communion" as "the body and blood of Christ" is not a part of Jewish teachings.

2. Plum Village is located in southwest France in the Bordeaux Valley, near the Dordogna River. It is a Buddhist village, where Thich Nhat Hanh lives in exile from his homeland in Vietnam. Although Thich Nhat Hanh began his practice as a Zen Buddhist, he has evolved his own expression of Buddhism, with more singing and joyful communion than in classical Zen.

Chapter Ten
"To Triumph over Evil" by Linda Thieman

1. In many Middle Eastern countries, job opportunities are not publicly advertised. Information is passed word of mouth among friends and family, and nepotism is very common.

2. This is historically accurate. Anti-Semitism was very common in ancient Rome. In addition, because he was a soldier and there were frequent Jewish uprisings against Rome, her master might have seen her as "the enemy."

3. Whitton, Joel L., and Fisher, Joe, *Life Between Life,* Warner Books, Inc., New York, 1986.

4. Jewish canon law requires a *minyan* or quorum of ten Jews in order to hold a worship service or say *kaddish,* the prayer for the dead. A *minyan* is also necessary for performing exorcisms. In Eastern Europe, it was common for a *minyan* to gather around the deathbed, to assist the soul in its transition to the next world. Many Jews believed that they could not go to Heaven unless someone said *kaddish* (prayer for the dead) for them. Although this is not strictly true, such a belief could hold a soul earthbound. Judging from the rest of the story, it would appear that the spirit *minyan* came to Thieman's house in order to say *kaddish* for souls that had been earthbound since the Holocaust. (At the time of these events, Thieman was not aware of these teachings.)

Chapter Eleven
"My Little Precious" by "Rebecca"

1. Not her real name. When I first spoke with "Rebecca" about using this story, she was willing to use real names but, because "Leah" is a minor, we later decided to use pseudonyms in order to protect her daughter's privacy. Both parents were also concerned that revealing "Leah's" name in a story about a past life as a Nazi collaborator might cause problems for "Leah" within the Jewish community.

2. This is historically accurate. Although normal bunk beds usually have only two levels, the barracks in the Nazi concentration camps had three or more. The famous photo of male prisoners lying in the barracks at Mauthausen (which includes Elie Wiesel) shows four levels of bunks. (See Lawless, Charles, *And God Cried: The Holocaust Remembered,* Wieser and Wieser, Inc., New York, 1994, p. 157.)

Chapter Twelve
"The Scapegoat" by David D. Johnson

1. This is not to imply that all Germans are abusive. However, as psychologist Alice Miller has pointed out in *For Your Own Good,* there were certain patterns in turn-of-the-century German child-rearing which often led to abuse. In some cases, these patterns have been continued in American families of German descent.

2. Although Nostradamus was officially a Roman Catholic, many scholars believe that he had Jewish ancestry. It is known that Nostradamus knew Hebrew and that he was rumored to have studied with Jewish alchemists in Narbonne, France (Cheethan, Erika, *The Final Prophecies of Nostradamus,* The Putnam Group, New York, 1989, p. 13). A recent television documentary suggested that Nostradamus derived his prophecies from the study of the Zohar, a Jewish mystical text (*Ancient Prophecies II,* NBC-TV, aired November 18, 1994).

3. Gershom, Yonassan, *Beyond the Ashes: Cases of Reincarnation from the Holocaust,* A.R.E. Press, Virginia Beach, Va., 1992, p. 24.

4. This refers to the Evenstar School of Sacred Paths, located at 2402 University Avenue West, St. Paul, MN 55114. Rabbi Gershom has periodically offered workshops there for over ten years.

5. See Leviticus 16. In biblical times, the scapegoat was a literal goat that was chosen by lot on Yom Kippur, the Day of Atonement. The sins of the people were symbolically placed upon this goat, which was then led into the wilderness to die. Nowadays, a "scapegoat" is anything which is unjustly blamed for the problems of others.

Chapter Thirteen

"A Dream of Infinity" by Mary (Miriam) Marks

1. See Silverstein's chapter, "The Healer Heals Herself," note 1.

2. According to Jewish religious law, membership in the community is matrilineal, i.e., passed down through the mother. A child born of a Jewish mother is completely Jewish, regardless of the father's religion. On the other hand, a child born of a Gentile mother is not Jewish, even if the father is. For this reason, Mary was required to go through a formal conversion in order to become a Jew. In more recent years, Reform Judaism has recognized patrilineal descent (a Jewish father and Gentile mother) as valid within their own fold, provided the child publicly identifies him/herself as a Jew and does not practice any other religion. Other branches of Judaism reject this stance, insisting upon formal conversion.

3. Named after Rabbi Hillel, a first-century Jewish sage who was renowned for scholarship and gentle patience. Most major American campuses have a Hillel center usually sponsored by the B'nai Brith Foundation and the local Jewish community. The Hillel center is both a religious and social meeting place for Jewish students.

4. *Yahrzeit:* the anniversary of a death. In Jewish tradition, the *Yahrzeit* is observed by reciting the *kaddish* (prayer for the dead) and lighting a twenty-four-hour candle in memory of the deceased. Many families also sponsor a religious feast on that day or the closest Sabbath. The *Yahrzeit* of a synagogue founder like Malka might also include public discussion and remembrance of her life and good deeds. According to kabbalistic teachings, the merit of the prayers recited and the Torah learned on the *Yahrzeit*

helps the soul to progress in the next world.

Chapter Fourteen
"Keepers of the Joy" by Patricia (Rachel Brachah) O'Brian

1. See Silverstein's chapter, "The Healer Heals Herself," note 1.

2. Deuteronomy 29:9-12.

3. According to the kabbalists, the souls who were at Sinai have reincarnated many times. Rabbi Elimelech of Lizhensk, a great Hasidic master, once said: "Not only do I remember how all the souls of Israel stood by the burning mountain of Sinai, I even remember what souls stood next to me." (Buber, Martin, *Tales of the Hasidim,* Schocken Books, Inc., New York, 1949, vol. I, p. 254. See also Gershom, *Beyond the Ashes,* pp. 73-75.)

4. The concentration camps were designed not only to kill the body, but also to break the Jewish spirit. In many cases, they more than succeeded. By publicly disdaining everything Jewish, the Nazis planted deep self-hate and shame on the soul level, which carried over into the present lives of many people, both Jews and non-Jews. For a more in-depth discussion of this phenomenon, see Gershom, *Beyond the Ashes,* pp. 143-150.

5. Unlike many religions, Jews do not have missionaries, nor does Judaism lure converts with promises of bliss. Traditional rabbis are required to discourage converts by pointing out everything negative about being a Jew. This "pushing away" is really a test of sincerity which, of course, cannot be explained to the seeker in advance.

6. I.e., prayer shawl and phylacteries. The *tefillin* are small leather boxes containing words of the Torah,

which are bound on the arm and head to symbolize binding one's thoughts and deeds to God. In Orthodox congregations, only the men use these items, while in the Conservative movement (O'Brian's denomination) women use them also.

Chapter Fifteen

"The Circle of Torah" by Yonassan Gershom

1. Gershom, Yonassan, *Beyond the Ashes: Cases of Reincarnation from the Holocaust,* A.R.E. Press, Virginia Beach, 1992, pp. 18-19.

2. Rabbi Nahum of Chernobyl (died 1798) was a disciple of Rabbi Israel Baal Shem Tov, the founder of Hasidism. At the time of Reb Nahum, Chernobyl was a well-known center of Jewish learning and is still mentioned in numerous Hasidic stories. Rabbi Goldberger's own teacher was the late Menachem Twersky, a Hasidic Rebbe descended from the Chernobyler's line.

Appendix A

"The Jewish Soul" by Rabbi Yonassan Gershom

1. Deuteronomy 5:3. For an in-depth discussion, see Gershom, *Beyond the Ashes,* chapter three, "The Afterlife in Jewish Teachings."

2. The "exile" can be a sentence imposed by the Heavenly Court as atonement for a specific sin, or it can be a voluntary act for any number of reasons. According to one classical Jewish source, "The souls of pious Jews sometimes pass [through reincarnation] into the bodies of Gentiles, that they may plead on behalf of [the people] Israel and treat them kindly." (Yalkut Reubeni 63) In all cases, the soul itself remains Jewish during the exile and eventually returns to its own people in a future life.

3. Fishkoff, Sue, "Endless Cycles: The Druse belief in rebirth can lead to complications," *Reincarnation International,* July 1996, p. 23.

4. From the videotape, "A Gift to One, A Gift to Many," courtesy of Min No Aya Win Human Services Center, Cloquet, Minnesota.

5. Iverson, Jeffrey, *In Search of the Dead: A Scientific Investigation of Evidence for Life After Death,* HarperCollins Publishers, New York, 1992, p. 176. Again, this belief is similar to that of many traditional Jews.

6. Because kabbalistic texts read "generations" as "incarnations," the idea of *yichus*—the "merit" of one's ancestors—can also be seen as a reference to one's own good karma. In this context, Rabbi Nachman's famous statement that " . . . even if I had come from the lowliest Jewish family, I still would have attained what I did" takes on new meaning (Shevachay Ha'ran 1:25).

7. Maller, Allen, *God, Sex, and Kabbalah,* pp. 121-123. On page 121, Maller states: "Of course, not all non-Jews who convert to Judaism are the reincarnated souls of Jews who were separated from Judaism in former lives. There is, however, one characteristic which hints at the identification of those who are: a single Jewish ancestor in their gentile [sic] family tree."

8. For example, the soul of the Panchen Lama, who has trained the Dalai Lama for nine incarnations, was believed "lost" after his death in 1989. But in 1995 the Dalai Lama announced that the Panchen Lama had been found—as a six-year-old Tibetan boy, the son of nomads in Chinese-controlled Tibet (*Reincarnation International,* London, July 1995, pp. 8-11). Note that the Panchen Lama came back immediately after his death and among his own people (like the Druses).

9. Traditional folk tale, also cited by Martin Buber in *Tales of the Hasidim,* Schocken Books, New York, 1947, Vol. II, p. 192. The same volume contains similar stories about the Apter Rebbe and Reb Levi Yitzchak of Berditchev (p. 120).

10. For example, see "Reb Nachman's Spirit," included in Howard Schwartz's *The Dream Assembly: Tales of Rabbi Zalman Schachter-Shalomi,* Amity House, New York, 1988, pp. 113-116.

11. *Op. cit.,* Iverson, p. 146.

12. In a letter to Edgar Cayce on July 6, 1939, a similar suggestion was made by client [813] about Hitler. Citing an astrological article published at that time, [813] suggested that the Nazis were being influenced by German souls who "died with hearts overflowing with hate" during World War I and were now either reincarnated or else influencing Hitler and his followers from the spirit world. Cayce's answer to this suggestion was that " . . . it is about right, am sure." (Reports 17 and 18 to reading 813-1)

Appendix B

"Did the Soul of Hitler Repent?" by Rabbi Yonassan Gershom

1. Gershom, Yonassan, *Beyond the Ashes: Cases of Reincarnation from the Holocaust,* A.R.E. Press, Virginia Beach, Va., 1992, pp. 233-234.

2. Schuster, Michael L., *Conversations with Adolf Hitler,* Sufra Publications, P.O. Box 997, Leicester, NC 28748, 1994, p. 355.

3. *Ibid.,* p. 15. Because "Old Michael" dropped out of Judaism in the ninth grade, his understanding appears to have remained on a teenage level. Since publication of *Conversations,* Schuster and I have discussed these ideas in more depth, and he is now com-

mitted to, in his words, "strengthening his Judaism once again."

4. *Ibid.*, p. 224.

5. As cited in *Shivchei Ha-Ari* (a sixteenth-century collection of tales about Rabbi Isaac Luria, a great kabbalist and mystic).

6. Brinkley, Dannion, with Perry, Paul, *Saved by the Light,* Villard Books, Random House, New York, 1994.

7. *Op. cit.,* Schuster, pp. 185-186.

8. *Ibid.,* p. 141.

9. *Ibid.,* p. 217. Compare this idea of spiritual "star systems" with the "healing centers" described by Abbye Silverstein in the opening chapter of this book, "The Healer Heals Herself." According to Silverstein, too, the astral bodies of the victims arrived in the interlife crippled and mangled, with their self-esteem severely damaged.

10. *Ibid.,* p. 101.

11. *Ibid.,* pp. 251-252.

12. Regarding my negative reaction to these claims, Schuster further explained to me: "The new age belief is that we all create our own reality, including the choice of our life circumstances before birth . . . Why would anyone choose torture? For the same reasons that others choose pain of any kind. Extremes of abuse are played out all the time in personal relationships. Why do the partners of these relationships remain in these abusive situations? To learn the lessons of self-love and forgiveness. The lessons are the same for the Holocaust victims." I still disagree with this theory.

Appendix C

"Edgar Cayce on the Holocaust" by Rabbi Yonassan Gershom

1. July 18-23, 1993, "Reincarnation: The Golden

Thread of Life," a conference sponsored by the Association for Research and Enlightenment, Inc., at their headquarters in Virginia Beach, Virginia.

2. Cf. reading 261-14. The 261 series provides an interesting window into the economic concerns of this period. [For the sake of privacy, all of Cayce's clients are identified by numbers. The first number of a reading indicates the person for whom the reading was given, while the second number indicates which reading in a series that person received.]

3. Reading 3976-13.

4. The Treaty of Versailles was signed in June 1919, ending World War I, which Germany had lost. The terms of the treaty were extremely harsh. Germany lost all of her colonies, a portion of her European territory, most of her iron and steel industries, and all of her military factories. Her army was limited to a small militia, and she was required to pay exorbitant war reparations to the victors. Although some of these provisions were later modified, the Treaty remained, "for Germans of all groups, a unique act of savage vindictiveness." (Taylor, James, and Shaw, Warren, *The Third Reich Almanac,* World Almanac, New York, 1987, p. 340)

5. Readings 1608-1 and 1562-1. See also Cayce, Edgar Evans, and Hugh Lynn, *The Outer Limits of Edgar Cayce's Power,* Edgar Cayce Foundation, 1971. In Chapter Seven, "The Nature of Psychic Perception," the Cayce brothers present a convincing analysis of their father's strange gift and the ways in which it sometimes got sidetracked by others in the room. Although the Hitler reading is not covered in *Outer Limits,* I believe that the same principles would apply here.

6. Reading 3976-13, paragraph 8.

7. Because the pronouns in this entire section are

a grammatical nightmare, it is difficult, if not impossible, to determine exactly who "they" are in each sentence. One could also argue that the reference to the "dictates of the activity of the director in affairs" makes the entire paragraph refer to Germans who had "wandered far afield," not the Jews! This rendering would fit well with another idea in the Cayce readings, namely, that the wicked "sons of Belial" from Atlantean times were reincarnating in the twentieth century. For my discussion of the Nazis as the "sons of Belial" returned, see *Beyond the Ashes,* pp. 221-232.

8. Reading 378-17, paragraph 10-A, given on November 3, 1933.

9. See report R-19 to reading 378-50. I have found no record of Cayce's response. I did hear once that Gladys Davis, Cayce's loyal stenographer, sent [378] a scathing retort, about how Cayce would never condemn a single person, let alone an entire group of people. The next report (R-20) in the same file contains a cross-reference to a reading for [378]'s daughter [457], given in February of 1939, in which she expressed concerns about inheriting insanity from her father's side of the family. Mr. [378] did have an insane sister, who died in January of 1938. This family history strongly suggests that [378]'s pro-Nazi letter was preserved in his file in order to document his mental state. On anti-Semitism as a form of mental illness, see Rubin, Theodore Isaac, M.D., *Anti-Semitism: A Disease of the Mind,* Continuum Publishing Company, New York, 1990.

10. Sklar, Dusty, *The Nazis and the Occult,* Dorsett Press edition, New York, 1989, p. 16.

11. Cf. Ross, Robert W., *So It Was True: The American Protestant Press and the Nazi Persecution of the Jews,* University of Minnesota Press, 1980, pp. 26-40.

See also report R-17 to reading 813-1, where a client wrote a letter to Cayce in 1939, lamenting "the way the American public has absorbed Nazi propaganda about the Jews."

12. Reading 3976-13, paragraph 8-A.

13. Deuteronomy 30:3-4.

14. Cf. reading 3976-15, paragraph 9, given on January 19, 1934. This was a general reading on "earth changes" and prophecies. Paragraph 12 of the same reading refers to "the reduction of one risen to power in central Europe to naught"—probably a prediction about the demise of Hitler. Note that this prediction was given only two months after 3976-13 (the Hitler reading), which supports my theory that the 1933 Hitler reading was off target.

15. From an audiotaped interview with Rabbi Zalman Schachter and Rabbi Michael Paley, recorded at B'nai Or House in Germantown, Penn., on April 10, 1983. Courtesy of Rabbi Schachter.

16. Reading 3976-13, paragraph 10.

17. Reading 257-211, paragraph 11.

18. Daniel 11:36-37.

19. Daniel 11:30-33.

20. See Exodus 19:1-9 *et al.* In later biblical passages, "the Covenant" sometimes refers to the physical Ark of the Covenant in the Temple. However, since the Ark contained the stone tablets with the Ten Commandments, it was also a representation of Sinai.

21. Daniel 11:35.

22. Zucker, Simon, *The Unconquerable Spirit,* Zachor Institute, Mesorah Publications, New York, 1980, p. 28.

23. Deuteronomy 31:7.

24. See reading 991-1.

25. Krajenke, Robert, *Edgar Cayce's Story of the Old Testament,* Edgar Cayce Foundation, 1973, Vol. III, p. 5.

26. For the record: I have been active in peace work since the 1960s, and I stood up for Palestinian rights at a time when it was career suicide to do so. From 1982 to 1990, I was a frequent panelist at many symposia on Middle East issues. "Swords into plowshares" is also part of the Jewish prophecies, from the book of Isaiah.

27. Weiner, Herbert, *9 1/2 Mystics,* Collier Books, New York, 1969, p. 296. Rabbi Abraham Isaac Kook (1865-1935) was both an Orthodox mystic and a political pluralist. Although he supported the Zionist movement—a rare and controversial stance for an Orthodox rabbi in his day—he also pleaded for tolerance. In recent decades, the writings of Rav Kook have been misused by certain right-wing factions in Israel in order to justify policies against the Palestinians. In my opinion, this was neither the letter nor the spirit of Rav Kook's teachings.

About the Contributors

LENA-MARIE BROMAN has worked as a holistic therapist in Uppsala, Sweden. Her reincarnation story was recently featured in *Reincarnation International* (London, 1994), and she has spoken on numerous panels and TV programs in Scandinavia. She is currently writing a book about her experiences and is studying for the priesthood in the Church of Sweden.

SIGRID DREYFUSS-MANELIS is a newspaper columnist in Baltimore, Maryland, and has been a talk show host for a major radio station. She holds degrees in journalism and psychology, and currently serves on the boards of directors for several mental health organizations. She is happy and busy in both her professional life and her private life as a wife and mother.

YONASSAN GERSHOM is a Hasidic storyteller and theologian, whose articles on Jewish spirituality have appeared in many publications and anthologies. He is the author of *Beyond the Ashes: Cases of Reincarnation from the Holocaust* (1992) and *49 Gates of Light* (1987). He currently teaches mysticism and Hasidic philosophy through the Institute of Adult Jewish Studies at the Minneapolis Talmud Torah.

JUDITH HART lives with her husband in Baltimore, Maryland, and is the mother of four boys. She works for the University of Maryland Medical Systems and has a part-time private psychotherapy practice. She is also an ordained minister.

MARCIA HOLLABAUGH is a professional musician and composer who plays both classical and contemporary works on cello and piano. She has also studied a wide range of religious and philosophical doctrines. A longtime resident of New Mexico, she loves the wilderness and frequently spends time outdoors in the foothills of the Sangre de Cristo Mountains.

DAVID D. JOHNSON is a mainframe computer programmer who lives in Edina, Minnesota. He is a licensed teacher in the Unity Church and describes himself as "a religious mystic who is devoted to understanding God's work in myself and others."

DIANA LUBARSKY resides in Westchester County, New York. She is married, the mother of three children, and has worked for thirty years in the field of geriatrics rehabilitation. In 1995, her Holocaust sculptures were shown at a major conference on reincarnation and near-death experiences in Baltimore, Maryland. She continues to sculpt on Holocaust themes whenever time allows.

CAROLE LOUIE holds a bachelor of science degree in interior design, which she has practiced professionally for twenty-two years. In addition, she is a Minister

Director for the Universal Brotherhood Movement, Inc., in Naples, Florida, where she teaches meditation, spiritual growth classes, and workshops on reincarnation.

MARY (MIRIAM) MARKS earned a master of arts degree from the University of Judaism in Los Angeles, California, while rearing three children. She retired early from her administrative position at U.C.L.A. for health reasons and soon afterward fulfilled a lifelong yearning to become a citizen of Israel. Today she is a prolific quilter who loves computer games.

DAVID MOFFATT is a professional writer, nature photographer, and poet. He is listed in *Who's Who in the Midwest* and *The International Who's Who in Poetry.* His most recent book is *Explorations in the Ordinary: A Backyard Naturalist Looks at Minnesota.*

PATRICIA (RACHEL BRACHAH) O'BRIAN has been interested in Judaism since early childhood. She holds a degree in international marketing from Bernard Baruch College and has worked as a sales representative in Bayonne, New Jersey. She currently plans to enter the Jewish Theological Seminary and become a Conservative rabbi specializing in hospice work.

"REBECCA" is a therapist who works with addiction and grief/loss counseling. She states: "I believe we have a twofold mission on earth. First, to know and realize our own life's purpose; and second, to share the knowledge we have learned, spreading light and wisdom on this planet of ours." She lives in Sydney, Australia.

ABBYE SILVERSTEIN holds a bachelor of arts degree (cum laude) from City College, New York. She attended a master's program in psychology and counseling at John F. Kennedy University in Oreida, California, and has worked as an addiction counselor and human resources specialist. She is currently studying acupuncture and works as a part-time medical assistant in Rockville, Maryland.

LINDA THIEMAN is a retired English teacher, who holds a master of arts degree from the University of Iowa. She has devoted her life to helping others find joy and healing, and is currently working on a series of light-filled children's books.

BRUCE WHITTIER is a licensed dairy goat-milk producer in Kingston, Nova Scotia, and a customer services manager for Home Hardware. Since the writing of his article for this book, he has opened the Baker House of Etheric Treasures, a new age shop where he now does psychic counseling and channeling.

About the Author

Rabbi Yonassan Gershom is a Hasidic storyteller, teacher, and writer. He utilizes techniques from Jewish mysticism to help seekers integrate traditional religious practices with personalized holistic consciousness.

Reb Gershom's work on Jewish spirituality has appeared in many periodicals and anthologies. He is the author of *Beyond the Ashes, From Ashes to Healing,* and *49 Gates of Light.* He is currently working on *Jewish Reincarnation Stories,* a collection of Jewish folk tales on the theme of reincarnation.

* * *

Due to the enormous amount of response to his work, Reb Gershom is no longer able to offer free phone consultations as described in *Beyond the Ashes.* He can be contacted by mail at:

Rabbi Gershom
P.O. Box 555
Sandstone, MN 55072

Enclose a long, stamped, self-addressed envelope for a reply, and please be patient—he receives a lot of mail. Messages can also be sent by Internet e-mail to:

rooster@pinenet.com
website: http://www.pinenet.com/~rooster/index.html